A CHARTERED
SUCCESS

Ian Ormes

GRANTA EDITIONS

© Britannia Airways Limited
London Luton Airport, Bedfordshire LU2 9ND, United Kingdom.

First published in 2002 by Granta Editions
25–27 High Street, Chesterton, Cambridge CB4 1ND, United Kingdom.

Granta Editions is a wholly owned imprint of Book Production Consultants plc

A CIP catalogue record for this book is available from the British Library.

ISBN 1 85757 078 2

PICTURE ACKNOWLEDGEMENTS
The author and publishers are grateful to the following for permission to reproduce photographs and illustrations:

Cover Adrian Meredith Photography; p.ii Adrian Meredith Photography; p.3, Don Tanton; p.5 'A fine night shot of a Euravia Constellation at Luton Airport', Don Tanton; p.11 'Luton's first terminal building', Philip Hodgkinson; p.21 Jean Bacon; p.32 Visual Impact; p.41 Visual Impact; p.43 'The cardboard bomber', Philip Hodgkinson; p.55 Jean Bacon; p.61 (inset) Ian Loasby; p.76 Guinness UDV; p.99 Adrian Meredith Photography

All other pictures were provided by Britannia Airways Limited.

Every effort has been made to obtain permission for the reproduction of the illustrations and photographs in this book; apologies are offered to anyone whom it has not been possible to contact.

Designed by Peter Dolton.
Design, editorial and production in association with Book Production Consultants plc, 25-27 High Street, Chesterton, Cambridge, CB4 1ND, United Kingdom.
Reprographics in Great Britain by HiLo, Colchester, Essex, United Kingdom.
Printed and bound in Singapore by Kyodo Printing Co (S'Pore) Pte Ltd.

Contents

Introduction   *ii*

Foreword   *iii*

1. Airborne   1

2. Groundwork   9

3. Britannia Britannia   19

4. A uniquely correct decision   29

5. Jet propelled   39

6. Turbulence   47

7. The orange factor   57

8. The battle to save the fleet   65

9. Flight plan   77

10. Flying – with confidence   85

11. A great airline and a great business   93

    Index   104

Introduction

FOR THE LAST FORTY YEARS, IT HAS been the people working for Britannia who have made the airline such a tremendous success. People have always been important, not just to the company but to colleagues within it as well. Over 70 per cent of our workforce has been with us for more than ten years. There is still a significant number who have been with us for more than 25 years. Britannia is very much a family-orientated business, with a remarkable number of wives, brothers, sisters and parents, working alongside other family members.

The spirit of this book, published to mark the fortieth anniversary of Britannia, reflects this family feeling. As the seventh Managing Director of Britannia, I have seen the airline move from the Thomson Travel Group family to the larger family of Preussag, within the World of TUI. This is the latest phase of the company's continually evolving story.

Britannia is one of the oldest continuous names in British aviation history, with a proud heritage built on strong values of safety, security, customer satisfaction and staff. These have been consistent throughout the last four decades.

I hope that you will enjoy this book which tells the story of Britannia through the eyes of the company's most important asset: its people. The people have contributed so much to the prosperity and longevity of this, the world's leading holiday airline. On our fortieth anniversary, I offer everybody who has been connected with our success story, my congratulations, best wishes and thanks.

Kevin Hatton, Managing Director.

Kevin Hatton

Foreword

IT IS HARD TO EXPLAIN WHAT IT FEELS like when you are standing on the steps of an aeroplane with your children and grandchildren and your close friends, and on the side of the 'plane is written your husband's name, *Bill Travers*. Could any of us have dreamed that the liaison between Britannia Airways and the work of the Born Free Foundation, begun in 1995 as a generous gesture to fly two rescued lions from rooftop cages in Tenerife to a sanctuary in England, would continue, undiminished, until the present time? And that out of this working relationship, though sympathetic from the outset, would develop a strong and loyal friendship?

The naming of the Britannia aircraft was in honour of Bill and all he had worked for, and achieved, in the field of animal welfare. A recognition of his passionate belief that wild animals do not belong in cages, that they deserve to live in their own natural environment and fulfil their own destiny. Bill had died in 1994 and as we all gathered at Gatwick Airport on that emotional occasion in 1999 there was, I felt, an even more personal and special bond established between Britannia and our Foundation.

I had flown with Britannia on several of their animal rescues, and the friendliness and support of the crew and staff had been heart-warming. Seeing many of them in their smart uniforms on that day, sensing that they too were experiencing the uniqueness of the occasion, created a feeling of extended family. And, of course, as the years have passed the mutual involvement in our projects has extended as well.

Virginia McKenna receives a bumper cheque from Cabin Crew – money raised by Britannia in its 'Spare Coins Save Lives' in-flight appeal.

Through the Spare Coins project and the in-flight appeals, presented by BFF friends and Patrons Joanna Lumley, Martin Clunes and Helen Worth, Britannia has helped fund many of our major initiatives. From a Chimp Island Sanctuary in Uganda, an Education & Rescue Centre at Shamwari Game Reserve in South Africa, Kenya's largest elephant relocation, a Wildlife Ambulance, to the Polar Bear Surrogacy programme.

But for me, at the heart of it all, have been the rescues. Lions, leopards and tigers who, thanks to the wings of Britannia, have flown from existences in pitiful deprivation to lives of happy compromise, where food is plentiful, veterinary care exemplary and they are treated with respect and understanding. How touched Bill would have been to know that his name was written on one of Britannia's winged messengers.

My warmest congratulations to everyone at Britannia on their fortieth anniversary year.

Virginia McKenna

1. Airborne

WITH A COMFORTING CLATTER AND in strict sequence, the four mighty 2200hp Wright Cyclone engines coughed into life and after a proper pause for checks and clearance, the rather ancient Lockheed Constellation – G-ARVP – taxied on to the seldom used 5432 feet long main runway at Luton Airport and prepared for takeoff under the control of Captain Peter Edwards and a crew of four.

The roaring engines soon lifted the empty tripled-tailed airliner into the skies above Bedfordshire and the crew positioned to Manchester's Ringway Airport. There they collected passengers for a flight to Palma via Perpignan in south-west France. The flight had left Luton at 9.30am on Saturday, 5 May 1962, took off again from Ringway at 11.10am and eventually returned to its wet and quiet base just before midnight. In a low-key but important way the flight marked a milestone in aviation history – the inaugural operation of Euravia, the forerunner of Britannia Airways, which was to become one of the biggest charter airlines in the world, and 'the start of a holiday' for millions of passengers now jetting to the sun in favourite spots around the globe.

These were pioneering days for the fragile commercial aviation industry and several airlines had been overcome by debts, cash flow problems and the constant need for business. The inaugural flight for Euravia – held on Cup Final Day when Tottenham Hotspur beat Burnley – was a brave move that had followed months of organisation and determination. Euravia, a name chosen because of the development of the European Common Market, started life with three ex-El Al Constellation 049 type airliners in 82-seat configuration, fully overhauled, plus some spare engines and parts all obtained for a giveaway price of £90,000.

The new airline also offered the job of Chief Pilot to **Derek Davison**, *then 39, who was a Training Captain with El Al and had flown with the RAF, British Overseas Airways Corporation (BOAC) and Pakistan International. His logbook showed an interesting collection of aircraft: Tudors, Yorks, Argonauts, Constellations, Britannias and de Havilland Comets.*

Pictured in Palma after the inaugural flight of Euravia are pilot Captain Peter Edwards and two Cabin Crew.

El Al agreed to my release and my first task was to carry out a number of test flights on the Constellations out of Israel before accepting delivery. I commanded all three deliveries and particularly remember one flight with Mike Forster as the Flight Engineer. We carried a set of crystals to change in the radio sets as we passed through Cyprus control area to Athens, to Italy and so to Heathrow. The flight took ten and a quarter hours.

The Constellation was known to us as the hydraulic monster in recognition of the amount of hydraulic pipe-runs in the aircraft – all prone to leaks. Passengers slipped on hydraulic fluid as they ran to board their aircraft – there was no seat allocation in those days.

Hordes of airmen rushed out with drip trays and placed them in position around the aircraft whenever we visited Lyneham in order to protect their nice new RAF white concrete.

The very experienced pilot **Don Tanton** *was recruited to Euravia in March 1962 as a Constellation Captain at a salary of £2425 per annum, with increments of £55 for each year of completed service. Earlier he had flown Douglas Dakota airliners with West African Airways.*

I had been flying Constellation 749s with Skyways of London for about a year when I read an advertisement in *The Aeroplane* magazine as I was positioning through Beirut. I rang Euravia in London; they put my name on the list and ten days later I called again when I was back in London. They had carried out some checks on my career and said there was no need for an interview; they sent me a contract in the post. There is no doubt that the Constellation 049s operated by Euravia were pretty tatty aircraft. We had plenty of problems with them, including on the second flight operated by the airline. I was flying 77 passengers from Luton to Barcelona and Palma. After 30 minutes' flying in rain the windscreen wipers packed up owing to a jammed motor, and at Barcelona the wheel brakes ceased to work. I couldn't take the passengers on to Palma and two days later had to fly back empty to Luton. The passengers were flown on to Palma by another aircraft.

The hydraulic leaks were a constant problem. At Manchester we were always put on the same parking lot because of the amount of fluid that poured from the aircraft. I recall a particular problem we had in Valencia when we discovered we could not start number four engine on one of the Constellations. We found that the flywheel would not engage with the crankshaft. I said to my Flight Engineer,

Captain Don Tanton and his son Nigel, also a Britannia pilot,
pictured shortly before Don Tanton retired.

David Brown, that we had, from time to time, the same problem in West Africa on the DC3 Dakotas, which had the same starting system. We used to overcome it by undoing a little flap in the engine, attaching a chain and meshing the flywheel with the crankshaft. David Brown spent more than an hour going over the engine and eventually found the flap together with a lever on the back of the flywheel. There was no chain but we realised that it meant that the engine could be started if we could engage the lever. Eventually we decided that I would energise the starter from the cockpit, with the ignition off, while David Brown stayed up in the engine and manually engaged the starter motor when it reached the right speed. It worked, and we were able to fly the aircraft back to Luton.

That was the sort of thing we did in those days to make sure that the aircraft, and the airline, kept flying.

The crew at that time consisted of two pilots, a Flight Engineer and two cabin staff. We navigated using radio aids, tuneable by the pilots, with directional needles. We used to fly at around 20,000 feet, and fully loaded with fuel and passengers we would climb at around 800 feet per minute. We cruised at 210 knots. At that height we could not avoid too much bad weather and that could result in some bumpy rides for the customers. We used to do a lot of flying on Visual Flight Rules (VFR) and going in to Palma, for instance, we would often start our descent over Barcelona so that we could get under any bad weather and see the island and the airfield. If we went overhead and then tried to land we would not be able to see through the weather and would have to turn round for a long approach; this all took time and money and the waiting customers were anxious to get home.

The first passengers were supplied with lunch boxes consisting, as far as I can remember, of things like chicken legs and salad. The crew had the same but it was served on a plate rather than in a box. Later we provided hot food, which was served to the passengers from the heating ovens – rather than cooking ovens.

Early appointments to the airline, made by Director Captain Jackie Harrington, included Sid Finnigan as Chief Engineer from Pan American, Marianne Allen as Chief Stewardess [sic], Ernest Hessey as Operations Manager and **Captain Roy McDougall** *as Deputy Chief Pilot. After distinguished service in the RAF, he flew Lancastrians with BOAC and later became a freelance pilot. At one time he was involved in evacuation operations in the Belgian Congo. He now lives in South Africa.*

LEFT Proudly displaying the Euravia livery is one of the airline's first aircraft, an ex- El Al Constellation 049.

BELOW A fine night shot of a Euravia Constellation at Luton Airport.

My last company, Air Safaris, like many other independents that winter, had gone to the wall. I was co-author of a set of charter navigation manuals and I went to sell them to Euravia.

It was January, bitter cold, my fourth month of unemployment. I entered this odd collection of offices in London and was directed upstairs. On entering one of two offices I met Jackie Harrington, an old colleague from the BOAC, who almost immediately asked if I would like to be Deputy Chief Pilot, recruit pilots for a three-fleet Constellation airline and write the Operations Manual. I would not be paid as a pilot until April and I could start next Monday. I had never flown the Connie. Beggars can't be choosers – so I accepted.

The Operations Manual was typed in my late wife's office. Together with another pilot, Frank Brown, I moved into a room above a pub in Luton, where we had a problem with the pub owner's Alsatian guard dog. This was solved by Frank rushing up the stairs shouting loudly and the dog took to its heels. The pub owner was not amused.

Between them, the Chief Pilot and Deputy Chief Pilot set about forging the aircrew into a fully professional unit, eliminating some of the 'traditions' that had evolved in charter flying and making sure that high standards were set and maintained. **Roy McDougall** *remembers:*

Derek really set an example and the crews were quick to pick it up. The Chief Pilot stamped out traditional malpractices of aircrew – he forbade the custom of the flight deck team being given brandies by a hostess on arrival at their home airport, known as the 'after landing drink'. Equally, if the Cabin Staff took so much as an apple from supplies after leaving the aircraft, Derek told them they would be fired immediately. He also stopped the old Spanish custom of crews being allowed to retain half their hotel allowance if they returned to the UK rather than staying overnight at distant outstations.

I think, in the end, this kind of discipline went a long way to building up the spirit of the airline.

Keeping the charter airline going meant long hours for the aircrew, explains **Don Tanton.**

There were few, if any, flying time restrictions in those days and we would regularly put in a 12-hour duty day, which was from 'report' to 'off duty'. Report was

BRITANNIA FACT

The airline handles some 130,000 tonnes of passenger luggage every year.

usually looked upon as an hour before the scheduled flight time and off duty as 30 minutes after landing.

The flights took a long while; Luton to Palma, for instance, was four hours, ten minutes as against one hour, 50 minutes today. Turnaround time at Palma was one hour.

The Constellations were good to fly but generally considered a 'man's aircraft'. They had hydraulically powered rudders but still needed a fair amount of physical effort. The pilots' position was quite small because of the tapered nose, and the Flight Engineer sat behind us.

Positioning aircraft and other flights meant a certain amount of time away but when I was back in Luton I used to stay at the flying club at the airport, which was an old RAF shed with a good bar and good beer. In the back they had ex-RAF beds and we could stay there for ten shillings a night. We were looked after by a lady called May who made us welcome and provided a fine breakfast, which was included in the price.

Euravia's version of the Constellation 049 had previously been modified for high-density five-abreast seating, carrying passengers in comparative comfort. The uncomplicated first flight only hit one snag, according to **Marianne Allen.**

The aircraft left Luton without any oxygen masks on board. I asked the handling agent for some when we arrived at Manchester but he could only produce one. Luckily they were not needed.

The May 1962 flight had been the culmination of an enormous amount of hard work for **Derek Davison** *and others.*

I stood with others near the old customs shed and watched the take-off. It was one of my proudest moments. We patted each other on the back and said, 'We've made it. There she goes.'

Chief Pilot Derek Davison, who was to become Managing Director and later Chairman of the airline.

There were similar thoughts from **Don Tanton.**

I think we all felt we were starting something new and exciting. There was a tremendous comradeship; we knew it was going to be tough but somehow it felt right and it felt as though it was going to work.

The inaugural flight coincided with some dramatic action by British United Airways, then the UK's largest independent airline, which on 4 May had sacked all its 530 engineers, who had embarked on a go-slow. Managing Director Freddie Laker refused to negotiate 'under duress' with the engineers and thousands of holiday flights were at risk. These were also interesting days for the country as a whole, with Harold Macmillan still Prime Minister, a 'pay pause' still in operation and President Kennedy revealing plans for an Atlantic economic partnership.

Government 'red tape' was blamed for the demise of several airlines but the founders of Euravia, and thus Britannia, had struggled through a mass of obstacles to achieve their objective – as we shall see.

2. Groundwork

WHEN EURAVIA WAS REGISTERED AT Companies House on 1 December 1961 it lacked certain basic requirements for an airline. It had no aircraft, no aircrew, no engineers, no airport to use – and was minus a licence to fly. It did, however, have a small group of determined men and a grand plan – which, as it turned out, was quite enough.

The idea for an airline formed in the mind of one of the travel industry's greatest characters, Captain Ted Langton, and was translated into reality by John Ernest Derek Williams (known to all as Jed Williams).

Vladimir Raitz *formed Horizon Holidays in 1949, and in his book* Flight to the Sun[1] *he describes some of the early characters of the British travel industry.*

The first of these was Captain Ted Langton. He was, even then (in the mid 1950s), nearing the age of 60, and had spent all of his working life in the travel business. Having started his career with Thomas Cook and Son, he left to form his own coach touring company called Blue Cars. Langton built it up into a major force in coach travel throughout Europe. After the war Blue Cars grew even larger and Langton sold it for a considerable sum to BET – British Electric Traction. Langton owned racehorses, nightclubs and restaurants and even bought an ocean-going yacht which he kept in the Mediterranean and on which he hardly ever sailed. Despite his lifestyle, the lure of the travel trade was too strong. Even though he had signed a contract with BET that prohibited him from forming a touring company for the next two years, Langton (whose title of Captain was entirely spurious unless it derived from ownership of a yacht) decided to ignore such a petty sanction. Six months after the sale of Blue Cars, and having recognised that an air charter was the way forward, he formed his new company: Universal Sky Tours. BET promptly sued Ted for breach of contract, and won. He had to hand over a sum of money which was a fraction of the original purchase price, and which Ted could dismiss as a 'fleabite'.

Universal Sky Tours started out with a mixed programme of stay-put holidays, mainly in Majorca and the Costa Brava, as well as a few air-coach holidays similar to our own. The holidays that Universal Sky Tours offered were downmarket affairs. The emphasis was on mass travel at the lowest possible prices, within the framework of the regulations. Although Ted's operation was pretty large in its first year, it did not worry us too much. Esoteric destinations like Corsica and Sardinia were not his style – and in fact his marketing policy was so differently pitched from ours that there could only have been the most marginal overlap between our clientele. In any case, in a market that seemed to be growing at a phenomenal rate, there was certainly room for more tour organisers.

Ted Langton operated a holiday system that booked all the flying. He also booked all the beds at a destination hotel for the whole summer season, forcing the price down. He discovered, however, that when airlines went bust, which they often did, passengers ended up stranded at a resort. On the other hand, he did not want to pay the seat prices demanded by state airlines. He decided the only answer was to start his own airline. By coincidence he met Aviation Consultant Jed Williams, who later organised the Constellation 049 airliners from El Al. On a flight back from Israel, where they had clinched the aircraft deal, the two men talked, and in Flying to the Sun[2] **Jed Williams** *detailed the Langton plan for the new airline.*

Langton talked to me at length for the first time. Aviation legislation had been transformed in 1960. To carry paying passengers one required an Air Operator's Certificate from the newly created Director of Aviation Safety – a man who had enormous personal powers, including the right to withdraw a certificate in the middle of the night without warning – and a licence for the particular service from a new Air Transport Licensing Board (ATLB). They issued licences having regard to the public need, the diversion of traffic from existing licence holders and fitness of the operator (except in matters of safety), particularly financial fitness.

Langton saw this legislation simply as a bag of tricks designed to entrench British European Airways and put people like himself out of business. I disagreed. We argued.

A plan by Langton to form the airline in Spain was abandoned, Jed Williams was appointed Managing Director, a small office in Piccadilly became the company head-quarters, and a share capital of £25,000 was announced, with £5000 provided by Jed Williams. Licences to fly became the first big hurdle and **Jed Williams** *detailed the problems in an article in* Flight International[3] *in 1963.*

In 1961 British aviation was a debacle. Independent airlines went out like lights and the loss for the year on the government-owned airlines, with all their glittering traffic rights, soared well up to the £50 million mark. In these circumstances the sanity of anyone who started yet another United Kingdom airline might reasonably be questioned; yet it was precisely because of the virtual collapse of one sector of British air transport in 1961 that Euravia was formed.

e two men responsible for the formation of Euravia, the 'highly professional' Williams (left) and one of the great characters of the travel industry Ted ngton.

Luton Airport's first terminal building was extended in 1962 to handle Euravia's holiday flights. It is pictured in 2002.

Universal Sky Tours, which estimated that its losses (direct, indirect and consequential) arising from past failures of British independents over the years might exceed £250,000, asked the question: 'Is it possible in the British environment for an airline to be viable and financially stable and to provide a safe, reliable service at the price our inclusive tour passengers will pay?'

The answer, given in November 1961, was a carefully qualified affirmative. In the last days of that year we submitted to the ATLB our first group of applications for B licences for the summer of 1962. A 'B' licence, held in conjunction with a tour organiser, is for a regular series of flights (e.g. every Friday morning to Palma) for the exclusive carriage of passengers for the tour organiser on a specified holiday, usually with provisions as to the cost of the holiday. The Board is required to satisfy itself as to the suitability of the applicant, with particular reference to financial resources, insurance arrangements and conditions of service of employees. These items were dealt with by private hearing and correspondence.

The Board dealt with the obligation to consider the need for the proposed services and the effect on other airline services at a public hearing on February 20, 1962. I found my first public hearing most interesting. The list of objectors read like a directory of British airlines. One objection was that the proposed charters would divert traffic from a proposed scheduled service for which no licence had been issued and for which no evidence had been heard by the Board.

Universal Sky Tours, as the tour organiser, was accused by a Board member of asking for licences for which it did not have passengers, or alternatively of trying to get passengers for flights for which it did not have licences, both of which I gathered were heinous crimes.

In subsequent hearings we had the opportunity of collecting many such charming paradoxes, but the tour operators are not always charmed.

In the event, most of the applications by Euravia were approved but **Jed Williams** *was unhappy with the system.*

What the Board is really doing is deciding which tour organisers will be allowed to fly by British airlines to which resorts. Even if such a decision was desirable, the Board is incompetent for this task; its terms of reference do not require adequate criteria for decision. The only possible effect of all this major facet of ATLB activity is to prevent people in the lower-income groups from having air holidays abroad, to divert British passengers to foreign charter airlines of varying standards of safety and to harass British airlines and travel organisations and render them economically less efficient.

Getting some of the new pilots up to speed on the 'Connie' also proved a problem. **Roy McDougall** *was one of those who took the Airworthiness Requirements Board (ARB) examination for the aircraft type – and failed.*

We were informed by the ARB that there were many variations of the Constellation and their examination was based on the type operated by a Gatwick airline. We should ask them to run a course for us.

Frank Brown and I duly drove to Gatwick, found the operations room, and the only occupant took me to the Chief Pilot's office. This was a short meeting devoid of good manners. I was shown the door and informed that we were competitors and could expect no help of any kind. Frank had taken advantage of the empty office to use his 'spy' camera to photograph all the boards displaying numbers of aircraft, trips and dates to be flown and dates of major checks.

My two years as a freelance pilot had produced many contacts and I was soon talking to an airline's Chief Flight Engineer suggesting he ran a course for about ten pilots, for cash, at his wife's beauty salon. We duly arrived at 1800 hours and received notes and four hours of instruction a night, including a mock examination. Hot money buys most things, and we passed our examinations.

A Constellation of Euravia pictured around 1963 with pilot and Cabin Crew including Gill Kirk.

By now Euravia found itself with licences, aircraft on their way from El Al, aircrew and business. But still no airport. First stop was Gatwick, where the Airport Commandant had seen airlines come and go and offered few, if any, facilities. Ted Langton suggested a visit to Luton, then famous for hat-making and Vauxhall, the British subsidiary of General Motors. Jed Williams and Jackie Harrington visited the airport and met **Bob Easterbrook***, then Air Traffic Control Officer and later the airport's Director.*

The story these two characters gave me – and obviously I was a lot more naive than I am now – was that they were consultants for a potential airline and they were evaluating a number of potential sites in southern England to establish it. I showed them round and they said the facilities were hopelessly inadequate.

I usually took sandwiches for lunch as there were no catering facilities at the airport but on this occasion I thought the two visitors meant business and so I rang the Manager of an aero engine company, one of the airport's tenants, and persuaded him to give Jed Williams and Jackie Harrington lunch. A few weeks later the bill came in, at 7s 6d each, and the airport accountant strongly challenged the exorbitant price.

Whatever their first impressions, the two Euravia men returned and were shown round again by Airport Commandant Peter Rushton, who emphasised the sound runway, the reasonable navigation facilities and a new hangar. This time they decided to go ahead and in his book The Story of Luton International Airport,[4] **Jamie Glass** *details the next moves.*

Flight crew and Cabin Crew from an early Euravia flight on a Constellation.

Gill Kirk in 1960s Cabin Crew uniform.

The terminal building was almost doubled in size as it had been anticipated that Euravia would be handling some 700 holiday flights at Luton during 1962. Euravia leased a quarter of the new corporation hangar, about 12,000 square feet. The extension to the passenger terminal was undertaken between January and April 1962 and Euravia started moving into its hangarage in February, allowing the airline the much-needed workshop space, stores and offices. The relocation was completed in March.

Of the airport's expenditure of over £303,620 for that year, some £200,000 can be accounted for by the capital cost of the hangar.

The arrival of Euravia's first Constellation shattered the rural peace of the near-by village of Caddington, a little under three miles west of the runway, but the sound of Euravia's aircraft was to become a very familiar one as the airline made Luton its main departure point, operations centre and maintenance base.

On completion of the terminal building, Euravia was feeding through almost 250 passengers each morning and evening. The terminal was bulging with even more passengers during the high season as Derby Airways and Autair routed their own traffic through the airport.

And so now the airline was in operation with three aircraft – G-ARVP, G-AHEN and G-ARXE – aircrew, although one or two still lacked uniforms, a home base and licences to operate. It was poorly financed and Jed Williams had to provide a personal guarantee for £5000 when a new engine was required. Fate, however, and the vagaries of the British aviation industry were to lend a hand. Writing in Flight International,[5] **Henry M. Berney** *tracked the developments.*

Euravia's formative problems and difficulties were soon overcome and the three Constellations operated a very satisfactory summer season. Following an appraisal of the first season's operations it soon became apparent that additional capacity was required, so the problem of further or new equipment was studied. In the autumn

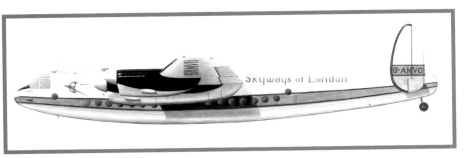

The October 1962 takeover of Skyways brought the Avro York into the Euravia fleet.

of 1962 the well-known and old-established independent Skyways suddenly found itself with a number of relatively modern Constellation 749s and insufficient work for their services. As the sole UK operators of Constellations, both Euravia and Skyways were thus faced simultaneously with equipment problems. Euravia, with only three aircraft, was faced with heavy seasonal traffic and limited capacity; Skyways, with three Constellations and four Yorks, and a general all-year-round business, had just lost, quite suddenly, the valuable BOAC contract to operate scheduled freight services between London and Singapore. Apart from scheduled passenger services between London, Tunis and Malta, and general charter work, Skyways' fleet was under-employed.

It was obvious to Euravia that, as the Skyways 749s had freight doors, these aircraft offered non-seasonal regular trade with the added advantage of the additional aircraft capacity so urgently required to meet the 1963 summer season commitments. The eventual solution was for Euravia to take over Skyways and the share capital was acquired in early October 1962.

The winter of 1962–63 found the now-established organisation concerned with problems of rationalisation and organisation. The fleet, which now consisted of six Constellations and four Yorks, was integrated at Luton, the Skyways aircraft moving over from bases at Heathrow and Stansted. During the winter months two further Constellations were acquired, both purchased from the former Trans-European Airways and delivered in 1963 to emerge in Euravia colours in time for the summer season. Major annual checks were carried out by Euravia, Marshalls at Cambridge and Israel Aircraft Industries at Lod.

The summer 1963 season saw Euravia operating a combined fleet of eight 82-seat Constellations on scheduled inclusive tour services to 12 regular holiday destinations: Tenerife, Valencia, Ibiza, Palma, Barcelona, Perpignan, Genoa, Venice, Rimini, Klagenfurt, Dubrovnik and Maastricht.

Euravia's financial situation presented some interesting challenges for **Bob Muckleston**, *who had joined the airline in November 1962.*

I had been working for the English Electric Company, based at Luton Airport. They were engaged in the production of ground-to-air missiles at the time and when the project was abandoned the unit was closed down. I was offered a position at their Stevenage office but decided to look for another job.

I had heard that a new airline called Euravia had set up at Luton Airport and that they were recruiting staff. They apparently needed someone to take over the

Bob Muckleston in the pre-fab offices of Euravia shortly after joining the airline at Luton.

financial side of the operation, among other things, and this sounded good to me. I applied and got the job.

Before getting to grips with the day-to-day running of the financial affairs of Euravia, I was required to spend time down at Lympne Airport [in Kent], closing down Skyways and transferring the accounts and administration to Luton.

So started my love affair with the airline industry, which lasted 30 years. Not that I had much faith in being able to build a career with Euravia. The prospects for the airline industry had been very poor since the war and as I finally had time to spend in the office after the absorption of Skyways into Euravia, I could see that the financial position of the company looked very shaky indeed. The turnover of staff was too high too and I remember sitting in my office thinking, 'This job will not survive six months.'

On my return to base from Lympne I was told that the Managing Director, Jed Williams, wished to see me. Jed was a man of considerable intellect and was very incisive and really quite different to any manager I had come across. Immediately after I sat down in front of him, he said: 'Muckleston, what sort of name is that? You can't forget that in a hurry.' It took me a while to work out what made Jed tick but we soon began to have a mutual respect for each other which lasted long after he left Britannia, and it was a sad day for me when I learned of his death from cancer in 1994.

His time at Lympne Airport had also shown **Bob Muckleston** *some of the rigours of the airline business.*

Skyways was in a mess. Due to their archaic system of handwritten books and credit control, it was difficult to find out exactly how much they owed. Their main source of income came from a scheduled service from Lympne to Le Touquet in France, and one to Malta, together with a stand-by cargo aircraft for Pan American Airways. They also had a maintenance facility at Heathrow.

I did, however, get a lot out of the time I spent with Skyways in that it was my first opportunity to see the workings of an airline, even if the airline was on the verge of bankruptcy. The airline had had a long and distinguished history and it was good to talk to the people there and get their input on the good and bad things that had gone on in the past. It always stuck in my mind that an absolute truth in business was that things always went wrong at a time when you could least afford it; therefore taking risks without substantial backup always spelt disaster. There were a number of things I saw at Skyways which I kept in mind and incorporated into Euravia/Britannia.

After the first 18 months, **Jed Williams** *produced an interesting breakdown of operations.*

Date	Number of employees	Fleet
15 January 1962	2	Nil
15 March 1962	4	Nil
15 April 1962	36	1 Constellation
15 May 1962	57	3 Constellations
15 June 1962	77	3 Constellations
15 December 1962	118	6 Constellations & 4 Yorks
15 July 1963	215	8 Constellations & 4 Yorks

1 *Flight to the Sun. The Story of the Holiday Revolution,* by Roger Bray and Vladimir Raitz. Published by Continuum, London and New York, 2001.

2 *Flying to the Sun. Quarter Century of Britannia Airways, Europe's leading leisure airline,* by Geoffrey Cuthbert. Published by Hodder and Stoughton, London, 1987.

3 *Starting a New British Airline,* by J.E.D. Williams. Published by *Flight International,* 7 February 1963.

4 *The Story of Luton International Airport,* by Jamie Glass. Published by Luton International Airport and Luton Borough Council, 1988.

5 *Airline Profile – Euravia (London) Ltd,* by Henry M. Berney. Published by *Flight International,* 5 March 1964.

3. Britannia Britannia

THE ACQUISITION OF SKYWAYS LTD, for just £1, meant that Euravia suddenly had a wealth of new assets, mainly aircraft. Derek Davison described it as a real turning point in the company's history, which signalled that the airline was here to stay.

The aircraft were a real bonus and even the less than beautiful Avro York freighters brought in some contracts. The airline's operating bases increased as it worked some of the Skyways routes, and many aircrew switched to Euravia. A downside, however, was that Euravia also inherited an overdraft of £250,000.

Within weeks of the September 1962 negotiated agreement with the receiver, the aircraft had changed livery and were being used for a variety of flights, not just package holidays.

Don Tanton, *who had left Skyways a year earlier to join the new airline, found himself back in the left-hand seat of the Constellation 749s, involved in a variety of 'out of season' flights including a complicated tour of Europe with the famous American ballet impresario Martha Graham, her dancers and her orchestra. She was a dancer, choreographer, teacher and director who developed the Graham Technique, which is now taught worldwide. She died in the late 1990s, aged 96.*

We also had another 749, flown by Jamie Alderman, which carried all the stage props and other equipment. We were gone for more than a month and before I left I was handed an absolute wad of money as we had to pay for everything by cash.

Captain Don Tanton (centre) with Cabin Crew Jo Falla, Pat Grainger and Jill Pollock, together with two members of the Martha Graham orchestra, pictured in Belgrade in 1962.

Quite where the airline found that money at that time I do not know. We even had to pay cash for fuel in many countries as a carnet was simply not accepted.

The stopovers included Athens, Belgrade, Zagreb, Warsaw, Munich, Cologne, Stockholm, Oslo, Helsinki, Amsterdam and Maastricht. We had a problem with an engine in Cologne, where we had a two-day stop, and eventually decided to fly the Constellation back to Luton on three engines. A new engine was fitted overnight while I slept at the flying club and then we flew back to pick the party up in the German city.

Martha Graham had the middle names of 'gin and tonic', and you can believe me when I say a fair amount of drink was consumed on the tour between November and December 1962.

The airline had been at some pains to make sure that it did not fall into the 'all the eggs in one basket' problem and at no time did Jed Williams allow Universal Sky Tours to account for more than 50 per cent of the bookings. The old Euravia aircraft had high operating costs and poor reliability and, despite everyone's best efforts, it was a struggle for the airline to make any real profit.

In Flying to the Sun[1] **Jed Williams** *explained some of the financial pressures.*

The problem was how to build up an airline without using money, and at the same time provide Universal Sky Tours with low-priced transport of acceptable standard to enable Langton to realise his plans. Those plans were, of course, important to us too, but they were also the only reason he formed the airline in the first place – and the source of the only interest he had ever showed in it.

Naturally, I consulted him about every major step but all he ever said was, at worst, 'I hope you know what you are doing', or, at best, 'You seem to know what you are doing.' Ted Langton was precisely the patron the airline needed in those days. He starved us of cash and was our most demanding customer. Within the restraint of these excellent disciplines, I could develop the airline as I pleased as long as nothing went seriously wrong.

The risk of something going seriously wrong on the financial side was, however, a little too close for comfort, as **Bob Muckleston** *discovered.*

The first major crisis I encountered was just before Christmas 1963. I was checking up on the finances of the company and found that we did not have sufficient funds to pay the staff their Christmas money – it was the intention to give this to them earlier than usual to help with the Christmas shopping. However, before giving this undertaking no one had thought about the cash flow implications. The other major outflow was that we had to make a standing payment to Israel Aircraft Corporation, which had sold us the aircraft.

One of the first signs of a company getting into financial problems is late payment of bills, but the last ditch of financial survival is when a company cannot pay its staff on time. At that period another airline was in trouble and we had started to have applications from their staff to join us, so if we failed to pay our staff on time then it could have started a run on us and lack of confidence from customers, which together could have been disastrous.

My choice was the staff or risk the Corporation removing our spares or worse, not returning spares which they had been repairing. I decided to pay the staff. During this period the financial position of the country was strained and there was a restriction of funds being moved out of the country. We had to go through exchange controls and money had to be placed in an external account with the bank who then had to apply to the Bank of England for permission to transfer the cash to the recipient. I lied to Israel Aircraft Corporation and said that the money had been lodged with the bank but it would be after the Christmas bank holidays before it would be passed out. I think that lie may very well have saved the airline.

A little twist of fortune suddenly added to the development of Euravia and gave it the chance it needed to meet all the demands of Ted Langton and Jed Williams. The story started 17 years earlier when BOAC was looking for a new medium-range 'Empire' transport aircraft and manufacturer Bristol Aeroplane Company eventually came up with the famous 'whispering giant', the four-engined turbo-prop Britannia airliner. It was not until 1957 that the Britannia 102 entered service with BOAC and also El Al. Later BOAC took delivery of the larger Britannia 312 series and immediately 'mothballed' its 102s. By 1963, with Euravia handling a rapidly increasing number of passengers, the search was on for replacements for the Constellations and Yorks. The 'mothballed' Britannia 102s solved the problems and Jed Williams bought six of the aircraft in a buy now, pay later deal. He also took the opportunity to dump the 'lousy name' of Euravia and rename the airline after the aircraft it had just acquired. It became Britannia Airways in the summer of 1964.

Derek Davison *remembers the changeover.*

We were very pleased to discover that the Britannia name was available for use by the airline. It was perfectly clear that British passengers liked the idea of flying a British airline; I am not saying they would have paid more for that privilege but it made them feel comfortable, particularly in the early days of inclusive tour holidays.

For a while, says **Don Tanton,** *the aircrew became 'ambidextrous'.*

After being converted to the Britannia we found ourselves flying both the turbo-prop and the Constellation for a few months until the Connie was phased out. Derek Davison and I became the first two pilots to convert to the new airliners, after a course with a man named Willie Williamson who was a Bristol Aeroplane test pilot. I did six hours 40 minutes by day and 50 minutes by night to receive my commercial rating for the airliner.

The Britannia was a fine aircraft to fly. The controls were a lot lighter than the Constellation but it could be difficult to land in a crosswind.

Meanwhile the Constellations were still plugging across the skies loaded with holiday-makers – and from time to time causing problems. A flight in April 1964 is particularly remembered by **Roy McDougall.**

Constellation 749 G-AHEN, known as the 'Hen', which had a reputation for being difficult and nearly brought about the demise of Roy McDougall, his crew and a full complement of passengers.

We were flying a Constellation we called the 'Hen' after the last three letters of its registration. The Hen had a reputation for being difficult. Our plan on this flight was to take one load of tourists to Munich, pick up American passengers for Rome and position empty back to Luton. Nice easy daylight work. Or so we thought.

*Captain Roy McDougall pictured in 1977 after being awarded
the Queen's Commendation for Services to the Air.*

On the second leg, Munich to Rome, Bill Brett was flying in the Captain's seat with me as Co-Pilot. We agreed that we should run through the emergency drills as our fleet was mixed, no two aircraft having the same cockpit configuration. Lovely blue skies, autopilot engaged, so a useful way to pass the time.

Approaching Rome, control had cleared us to 8000 feet – Bill disengaged the autopilot by pushing the three levers forward and was hand flying. I did notice that every now and again Bill was trimming forward to maintain level flight. Everything normal, or so we thought. Passengers strapped in, cabin ready for landing. Suddenly I heard a 'thang' sound and the aircraft began diving. Having just practised our emergency drills, I concluded that the hydraulic power had malfunctioned, overpowering normal controls, and must be disengaged. 'Let go Bill, you must let go,' I yelled. Bill released the control column; I pulled the walking arm to disengage hydraulic power, which should rectify the situation. But the angle of dive got steeper.

Whenever aircraft crash, a familiar criticism is 'Why didn't the crew call?' I had programmed myself that I would always speak, so I pressed the transmit button, 'Mayday, Mayday, Mayday. Diving, diving, diving.' Not even a dickey bird answered. We were approaching near vertical, the ground had stopped moving. My last memory was grabbing the control column wheel and yelling, 'Pull, Bill, pull.'

What happened next, I can't tell you. The mind has the trick of switching off the memory when 110 per cent concentration is required. The next I remember is the aircraft climbing at far too steep an angle and I was frantically winding the trim wheel forward. Convinced that we had faulty controls, I continued to manoeuvre the Hen by use of the trim wheel only. I decided I must inform control in case we dive again.

'Control, do you have a tape?' I repeat the message because they could not understand and eventually get the unforgettable answer, 'If you are thirsty we have many taps on the ground.' I give up and concentrate by flying by wheel trim only, and land. We 'phone the company, explain what has happened and then wait until the next day, when an engineer is flown out. He says the controls are working normally but our right undercarriage door has blown off. This deprives us of fire protection should the engine burst into flames. I suggest, and the company agrees, that I can use four engines for take-off and when safely airborne, shut down and proceed on three, starting the fourth again for landing. It worked well but approaching Luton, the engine would not start, so we landed on three.

Two days later Derek Davison and myself did a test flight, Derek flying. We got to 8000 feet, engaged the autopilot and went through the procedure we followed on our way to Rome. Nothing happened but on the third occasion the same noise and we went off into a dive. This time the recovery was quicker and the cause was the autopilot remaining engaged when the lever showed disengaged. This may have explained some other crashes with Constellations for which there were no ready explanations.

Ex-BOAC Bristol Britannia 102, G-ANBJ, which was delivered to Britannia Airways in April 1966.

The newly named airline was developing fast. In 1962 it had carried 20,000 passengers, by 1963 that figure had risen to more than 60,000, and the Britannia 102s would help boost the figures to more than 130,000 in 1964. In an article in Aeroplane,[2] *journalist* **Michael Lumb** *looked at the early days.*

Things moved swiftly in the airline right from its inception. Williams had seen the inevitability of finally going jet, but both the Connies and 102s had the advantage of being the cheapest investment possible, while giving the required capacity. He had dabbled – like any ambitious non-scheduled operator does – with the idea of freighting and scheduled services. But as he said at the time, he was 'far too busy managing an explosive expansion into the relative void of IT work' to progress the schemes very far.

The vagaries of the British and European aviation industries were a constant problem to those who worked in the business. Still in his teens, **Bernard Newton** *had joined the engineering department at Euravia helping to look after the Constellations and Yorks.*

In 1965 Britannia sold three Constellations to Ace Freighters and I was offered promotion to Charge Hand if I went to the new company with the Connies. After a while Ace Freighters went bankrupt and I was out looking for another airline. Over the years I worked for some six airlines, all of which disappeared for one reason or another, including Autair, Transglobe and Donaldson. There really was nothing unusual about these companies going belly-up; it was almost the norm, and the fact that Euravia/Britannia kept going is a remarkable achievement.

It was a precarious business and we came to expect airlines to go under for one reason or another. On one occasion I was travelling abroad with an airline and when we landed back at base we were told that the company had gone out of business; on another occasion I turned into work to be met in the car park by the Chief Engineer saying 'Don't bother'.

But as one airline closed another started up, so there was usually work available, and I must say that I learned one hell of a lot about aviation and aircraft by working in so many airlines.

The Britannia 102s could carry 117 passengers at a cruising speed of 375mph. They were fully pressurised, and much appreciated by passengers, not least because a hot meal, nearly always a cottage pie, was provided in flight. The aircraft were also well received by the ground handling agents. **Eric Nobbs** *had joined Manchester Airport*

Agencies (later Servisair) in 1957 and spent his first three years in Manchester before moving out to the city's airport.

Euravia began operating the Constellations to Manchester in 1962 and they used the old Ringway Airport. Two or three years earlier the airport had seen the upturn in holiday flights, known as inclusive tour flights in those days, and they were proving more and more popular.

The Connies were lovely aircraft, very good to look at, but they caused plenty of problems for us. The hydraulic fluid was everywhere and as the aircraft sloped from forward to aft when it was on the ground, the fluid ran along the whole of the underneath of the fuselage. On the Constellation the hold entrance was underneath the aircraft, which meant that the poor chaps who were caught for loading and unloading the baggage were constantly covered in hydraulic fluid as they climbed in and out of the hatch.

Believe me, when the Britannia Britannias arrived on the scene we were very pleased to see them.

We had started handling Euravia from the very start of their operations. We looked after their passenger handling at 'front of house' as it's known; we organised loading and unloading, cleaning, catering, weight and balance processing, provision of ground power and a variety of other tasks.

I was only just 20 when I arrived at the airport and I was mad keen to be involved in everything. They had built the new air traffic control tower and other operational buildings at that time; the terminal was developed later. It was still quite a small airport and everybody knew everybody.

I knew most of the Euravia/Britannia pilots and there were plenty of characters among the aircrew, particularly Jamie Alderman, who was a very fine man. I remember him flying out of here in a Constellation which rapidly developed engine trouble, and he had to fly around for a long while to reduce the fuel on board before he could land back at Manchester. There was a fair amount of concern at the airport as he landed on three engines. I said to him later that the landing must have been pretty hairy in those conditions. He said: 'I don't know, I had my eyes shut at the time.' In the early days it was largely a summer operation, and the aircrew and the number one hostesses were coached up from Luton on a Friday evening. The other Cabin Crew were recruited locally.

Many of the Captains were ex-RAF and were fairly laid-back about matters. If they were ten minutes late on landing there was no great concern – except that the aircrew were slower getting to the bar.

Britannia had a small engineering operation here at Manchester but if there were major problems it meant whopping delays for passengers. Sometimes an aircraft would have to be flown back to Luton for repairs, or sometimes parts would have to be sent up by road. On the whole passengers accepted the problems; they were put up overnight in a hotel, which usually pacified them.

By the mid 1960s the once-exclusive right of the wealthy to travel abroad for their holidays had gone. In the summer of 1965 more than three million passengers travelled on 50,000 inclusive tour flights from British airports. It meant, said **Travel Trade Gazette**, *that the 1950s were gone.*

For pleasure purposes, more people from more countries visited each other, by more ways and more routes than ever before. The jungle of red tape which hinders the easy freedom to travel has begun to be cleared away.

For Britannia the year was to see even more developments as it eased towards a premier position in the market.

1   *Flying to the Sun. Quarter Century of Britannia Airways, Europe's leading leisure airline,* by Geoffrey Cuthbert. Published by Hodder and Stoughton, London, 1987.
2   *How Britannia Counted the Cost,* by Michael Lumb. Published by *Aeroplane,* 31 May 1967.

4. A uniquely correct decision

AS GROUP DEVELOPMENT DIRECTOR of the Thomson Organisation, Gordon Brunton, now Sir Gordon, found himself with a major problem on his hands. His boss, media tycoon Roy Thomson, had presented him with the awesome task of looking at diversification for the organisation, well away from its television, newspaper and magazine empire but with a linked synergy if possible.

Gordon Brunton, who had rapidly progressed through the organisation, was looking for a young industry, which could employ some of the resources already in the organisation, could provide a different cash flow and would not be too technically demanding.

By research and analysis he came upon the package holiday industry, which was in its infancy and had the potential for massive development.

In his book Flight to the Sun,[1] **Vladimir Raitz** *looked at the background.*

Gordon felt that the package tour business would dovetail perfectly with Thomson's other interests. Holidays were paid in advance at a time of the year when newspaper revenues tended to be low and, conversely, the holiday bills [by the holiday companies] had to be paid when newspaper revenues were high.

Gordon asked me if I would sell Horizon Holidays to Thomson's and go there to run a newly formed Thomson travel division. He suggested that Horizon, being the premier upmarket tour company, would fit in particularly well with such Thomson newspapers as *The Times, The Scotsman* and the *Western Mail.* It was part of Gordon's plan that the newspapers could deliver millions of messages each week at a marginal cost to promote the company's travel interests and give them an enormous advantage over the competition.

I was greatly surprised by Gordon's proposal – as well as intrigued and even flattered. However, it didn't take me long to decide that I valued my independence too much to become part of a huge organisation like Thomson's, however tempting the financial inducements.

Vladimir Raitz did, however, offer to help in the search for a suitable company for Thomson and rapidly suggested Universal Sky Tours, which had a controlling interest in Britannia Airways. He approached the chain-smoking Ted Langton, who was immediately interested in the offer. Meetings took place and 'due diligence' enquiries carried out by auditors. Their report, however, was 'totally negative', said **Vladimir Raitz.**

According to the report, financial control was non-existent [at Universal Sky Tours]; the company was running at a loss, there was no coherent management structure whatsoever and every decision was taken by Captain Ted himself. The only positive aspect was Euravia (Britannia), which was professionally run by Jed Williams, an old aviation hand. But the airline at that time was a relatively small part of the whole.

At a Thomson board meeting, Gordon Brunton remained positive and said he was absolutely confident that the time was right to enter the industry that was poised for explosive growth.

In his book After I was Sixty,[2] **Roy Thomson (later Lord Thomson)** *wrote of the decision to buy into the industry.*

The project was presented to us by Gordon Brunton in the boardroom at Elm House. He had called the accountants to examine the balance sheets and the projections, and to give their views of the proposal. We had found an opening in the travel business fairly early in its developing story; this can be judged by the fact that Sky Tours had not yet shown a profit. Nor were there any assets other than three or four Britannia aircraft. Only goodwill and shrewd faith. I don't think I have ever heard a less favourable report than what the accountants gave that day. In our three hours' discussion, a great deal was said about what could go wrong with Gordon's scheme. I did not say anything until all this had been aired, and then I said I wanted to go ahead with Gordon's proposal. 'I think he may be right,' I said. Our Marketing Director raised some doubts about including an airline in the scheme. He had the idea that ordinary people would not go for aircraft travel. We went into the travel business.

Thomson bought Universal Sky Tours and at the same time bought the smaller company Riviera Holidays. In the purchase, however, **Gordon Brunton** *had to deal with the wily Ted Langton.*

We paid £300,000 for Universal Sky Tours, largely based on Ted Langton's projection of the season's trading, but Langton was concerned that the company might do much better in the future and he wanted an additional payment based on performance.

Gordon Brunton (later Sir Gordon) and Lord Thomson, the men responsible for adding Britannia Airways to the Thomson portfolio.

EMERGENCY EXIT

G·ANBO

BRITANNIA

I said that if I agreed to that, would he also agree to refund me if the company did worse than predicted. Of course, he declined. We discussed the matter and eventually we agreed that we would pay extra performance-related monies up to a total of £1 million. We shook hands. I think he thought I was a fool.

In the first year we made a £1 million profit and if he had not agreed to the ceiling he would have been paid a great deal more.

Gordon Brunton's *dramatic plan for the Thomson Organisation was under way.*

Having bought Universal Sky Tours, I started with an assumption that I disliked businesses that are vertically integrated. Being a publisher that owned a variety of newspapers and magazines, I did not like owning the printing works that were used for the publications; if anything went wrong, we were in for a double whammy – both the publications and printing works would be hit. And that's why, when I joined Thomson, I was instrumental in selling off the printing operations; we could then be totally independent and go where we wanted for the best printing deal. When the downturns came we did not take a double whammy.

For those reasons I decided, when we bought Sky Tours, that I did not really want to be in the airline business. Vladimir Raitz of Horizon, and other companies

Lord Thomson is welcomed onboard by Captain Don Tanton.

like Riviera Holidays, were all buying their flights in the cheapest market and that seemed the best option. I could not see an advantage for having expensive hardware lying around on runways waiting to be used.

But after a while I realised that I was wrong and that it was absolutely essential to have a totally integrated operation where we could plan every aspect, and it became obvious that the airline was part of the profit centre.

I did, however, insist that neither party subsidised the other and that they stood on their own feet, and if the package tour companies could buy their air operations cheaper than Britannia, they had a right to do it.

At first the package companies used other airlines but after a while they realised that they could not do any better than Britannia and the business flowed that way.

Britannia became a wholly owned subsidiary of the Thomson Organisation in April 1965; by August that year the last Constellation was withdrawn from service and the summer fleet consisted of five ex-BOAC Britannia 102 aircraft – G-ANBO, G-ANBF, G-ANBA, G-ANBL and G-ANBB.

Disposal of the earlier aircraft provided some interesting moments for **Bob Muckleston.**

We managed to sell some of the Connies to Spain but no one wanted the Yorks, so they went to the breakers. Obviously as the aircraft were mainly alloy frame-work and had plenty of useful equipment and other materials, there were scrap merchants who were interested in doing the job. Unfortunately they were not very savoury people, as I found out to my cost. Some of the most notorious criminals in London were involved in the scrap business. The firm we finally chose to scrap the Yorks seemed to be respectable and started on the job well and disposed of the aircraft. They had paid some of the money up front and I waited for them to pay the balance. The money did not come. I then contacted a debt collector who went to see them. He could not find anyone there. Shortly after, I had a visit from the police, who asked me who had removed the aircraft. They turned out to be one of the most vicious of the London gangs, and the police advised me to stay well away from them. I wrote off the debt!

As Chairman of Britannia Airways Limited, Gordon Brunton was looking forward to a period of consolidation within the organisation. Before the acquisition, Managing Director Jed Williams had at least indicated that the Britannia airliners would suit the airline for years ahead. But things move fast in aviation and within a few months of the takeover, Jed Williams had a new plan which he presented to **Gordon Brunton.**

Jed and his team had heard glowing reports about the Boeing 737 jet airliner and suggested that we should consider the possibility of buying them for Britannia. He made a good case, and it was also obvious that something was needed to modernise the airline and help it provide the service that was required by the package tour holiday companies.

The man charged with looking at the possible introduction of 737 jetliners into the airline was Britannia Projects Manager **Peter Swift,** *who in November 1965 presented a detailed report to the airline's board. It showed passenger miles increasing from 27 million in 1962 to 184 million in 1965 and a projected 258 million in 1966.*

This growth has been largely associated with the growth of Universal Sky Tours in a joint operation, the success of which has simply depended on offering the public a better buy in terms of price and quality of service.

There is no reason to believe that the future growth rate of Britannia Airways could not be 40 per cent per annum (i.e. doubling every two years) provided we continue to maintain two key features. These are integration and coordination of planning with the associated tour organiser and very low-cost operation.

And dealing with the 737, **Peter Swift** *explained:*

Boeing have made a 'breakthrough' in operating costs with this aircraft, which means that even at low utilisation the 737 is still more economical than current types. Basically the Boeing achievement is to produce at a low price an aeroplane which can carry 117 passengers over 1000 nautical miles using only two JT8D engines and taking off at 97,000lb – the gross take-off of the four-engine 82-seater Constellation.

This breakthrough in operating costs happens – by coincidence – to have been achieved on an aircraft with identical capacity to the Britannia 102 so that the vehicles are interchangeable.

A typical 737 schedule for the peak summer inclusive tour programme, shows that three return trips to a Mediterranean resort can be carried out per aircraft per day and still permit suitable times for passengers to arrive and depart, making use of public transport both to arrive at and depart from the London terminal.

Britannia Cabin Crew member Sue Lloyd adding a touch of glamour to one of the two turbo-fans on a Boeing 737-200.

The report indicated some options to the board, including staying with the Britannia fleet, buying further 'obsolescent' aircraft and waiting to see if a new aircraft giving lower seat mile costs came on the market, but basically the conclusion was 'buy Boeing'.

The purchase of three Boeing 737-200 series aircraft immediately is a uniquely correct decision.

That recommendation set in motion a whole series of events and put **Gordon Brunton** *under enormous pressure. By 1966 Harold Wilson's Labour government, which was struggling with a variety of economic problems, had reintroduced currency restrictions and limited Britons to £50 of foreign exchange when they travelled abroad. The government was also strongly pushing a 'buy British' campaign.*

The Boeing 737 was new, was largely unproved, and at first it was difficult to sell the idea to the Thomson board. The alternative to be considered was the BAC One-Eleven, which was well used and well known and was British.

Jed Williams, however, was adamant. He felt the aeroplane for Britannia was the 737, which was tailor-made for the short- and medium-haul market.

At BAC in Weybridge, Surrey, Managing Director Sir George Edwards and his team felt that the series 300 and 400 One-Elevens, powered by two Spey 511 engines, capable of carrying 89 passengers over 1420 miles at a cruising speed of 540mph, were the ideal aircraft for Britannia. Versions had been sold to British United Airways, Braniff International Airways, Aer Lingus and Court Line. Presentations were made to Britannia but Jed Williams and the team, including Peter Swift and Technical Manager Jimmy Little, still wanted the 737. Again it fell to **Gordon Brunton** *to consider.*

I decided to bring in a totally independent consultant. So I asked Steve Wheatcroft, a former Commercial Director of British European Airways who had later set up his own consultancy, to help. He spent a while looking at the options and his firm recommendation was that Britannia should buy the BAC One-Eleven.

Jed and his colleagues argued very strongly that the recommendation was wrong. Sir George Edwards and his team then made another presentation to me; the Boeing people came back and made another presentation. On top of everything else, I was under enormous political pressure, particularly from Tony Crosland (then President of the Board of Trade), who said that it was my patriotic duty to buy British.

Before we made a final decision, Sir George Edwards said that if we worried about capacity etc., he and the BAC team would come up with a proposal for a stretched One-Eleven. He promised a response within ten days. At the end of that time he came to see me again and said that they were not able to stretch the 300 series as he had thought. The two of us sat there. He was a tough but pleasant man, very direct and straightforward. I explained that as far as I could see, the answer for us was the 737. Then he admitted to me: 'I can't compete with the 737 but I will fight you all the way.'

The political pressure continued and Crosland told me that if I bought Boeing they would levy an import duty that was normally excluded for airlines. They then put pressure on Roy Thomson to try and persuade me to buy British.

The first Boeing 737-200 delivered to Britannia Airways nearing completion in Seattle. The aircraft – registration G-AVRL – was named Sir Ernest Shackleton.

He said he would back me to the hilt, whatever decision was made. Eventually the decision was made – and I told the board that we wanted to buy the Boeing 737.

It was probably one of the best decisions I ever made in my life. Everything Boeing said about the 737 was right and in most cases it exceeded expectations. It was a magnificent aircraft and the key to the success of Britannia Airways.

Jed Williams and his team showed courage and intelligence in sticking out for the 737. It was, in my view, one of the major reasons for the success of Thomson and the advantage it gave all our tour companies in a brutal competitive period.

The Labour government stuck to its threat and imposed duty on the import of the Boeings, the first of which – G-AVRL – entered service with Britannia in July 1968. The financing of the aircraft included 80 per cent of borrowing, some US\$12.4 million from the Boeing Company and the Export-Import Bank of Washington.

Flight International[3] in April 1967 reported on the Barnwell Memorial Lecture given in Bristol by Jed Williams. It reported his views on the pressure the airline had been under when buying Boeing.

Mr Williams said that the air transport and manufacturing industries had a common interest, with the strength of one supporting the other, but the views that British manufacturers should build for a British airline, whether the rest of the world wanted the aircraft or not, and that a British airline should buy the wrong aircraft simply because it is British built, were 'sick and decadent'. A policy rigidly based on such views 'reduces both industries to impotence'.

1 *Flight to the Sun. The Story of the Holiday Revolution,* by Roger Bray and Vladimir Raitz. Published by Continuum, London and New York, 2001.
2 *After I was Sixty,* by Lord Thomson of Fleet. Published by Hamish Hamilton, 1975. Reproduced by permission of Penguin Books Ltd.
3 *Learning from Past Mistakes,* by J.E.D. Williams. Published by *Flight International,* 20 April 1967.

5. Jet propelled

WITH BOEING 737s ORDERED FOR the airline, and Britannia now a vital cog in the Thomson Organisation, Jed Williams decided that the time had come to relinquish his role as Managing Director.

A small and highly efficient management team, including Technical Director Jimmy Little, Financial Director Bob Muckleston and Derek Davison, who had become Operations Director as well as Chief Pilot, made sure that the airline and its eight Britannia aircraft continued along the right path, and the search started for a man to replace Jed Williams.

As fate would have it, the Chief Pilot of Harold Bamberg's British Eagle airline was looking around for a new career and had approached the Luton-based airline. He was Seychelles-born John Sauvage, who had served with the illustrious Pathfinder squadrons of Bomber Command during the Second World War, earning himself the Distinguished Service Order together with the Distinguished Flying Cross and Bar. He had spent some 16 years with British Eagle after the war and was extremely well known in aviation circles as a highly proficient pilot and organiser. After meetings with Gordon Brunton and Sir Miles Thomas, a former Chairman of BOAC who had joined the Thomson Organisation board, **John Sauvage** *was offered the job and became Managing Director in February 1967.*

They were still pioneering days for the aviation industry and in truth Britannia was considered a small airline. It was quite busy in the summer months but very, very slack during the winter, so much so that Jed Williams had considered closing down the airline during the winter months.

One of my first tasks was to look at this problem, and an area I considered was the possibility of trooping flights for the Ministry of Defence. With the imminent arrivals of the 737s the prospects looked good but there were some detailed negotiations ahead before the contract was secured.

The airline management was very strong. It had been called a 'pilot's airline', and it was certainly true that many of the management team in key positions were either pilots or ex-pilots, but that helped the operational strength of Britannia. Derek Davison, for instance, had built a strong operations division, one of

John Sauvage became Managing Director in February 1967.

the best in any airline. And the maintenance section under Jimmy Little was extremely strong; he had gathered a really good team that built the foundation for a lot of future development within the airline.

Founder Jed Williams moved from Managing Director to Chairman but by June 1967 had decided to take full retirement, and his place was taken by Sir Miles Thomas. **Jed Williams** *told* Flight International[1] *in that month:*

Lord Thomson and his colleagues have always treated me with the greatest consideration, never interfering with Britannia Airways, and when I wanted nearly $20 million to buy American jets they backed me unhesitatingly. It is just that, reaching last year the mid-point of a normal adult working life, I decided that this was not what I wanted for the second half. I have been working for months with my closest colleagues in Britannia and with the Thomson Organisation to get Britannia into the right posture and with the right industrial structure of Thomson Industrial Holdings to be able to realise the full potential of the airline. In my opinion Britannia and its present team have a value second to no independent in Europe.

A few months earlier the other man responsible for the founding of Euravia/ Britannia, Captain **Ted Langton**, *had also stepped down, as Managing Director of Universal Sky Tours, then the UK's biggest air holiday company. He gave no reason for his departure but told* Travel Trade Gazette[2]:

All I can say is that I haven't fallen out with Thomson and they haven't fallen out with me.

The management changes in 1967 had followed a tragic autumn in 1966 when Britannia G-ANBB, with 110 holidaymakers and seven crew on board, crashed on the approach to Ljubljana Airport in Yugoslavia, with the loss of 95 lives. Immediately the tragedy was reported, Derek Davison and a team of Britannia staff flew to the crash site. The airline's then Chairman, **Gordon Brunton**, *together with his wife and family, was on his way back home from a holiday on his boat off Majorca.*

When I arrived at Palma Airport I was greeted by Britannia staff with dejected faces who told me the aircraft had crashed. I flew straight to Luton and immediately flew back to Italy and collected a convoy of vehicles and people who could help, and drove directly to Ljubljana.

It was a very difficult and grim time for us all. The little burns unit at the local hospital was doing a magnificent job. It may normally have handled perhaps one patient a week or a month, and suddenly had this influx of people needing urgent help. They worked round the clock for two weeks treating the badly injured. Their equipment was a little outdated and I arranged for special equipment to be flown out from the UK to help the doctors in their work. They needed a variety of special equipment and drugs and it was largely provided by hospitals in London. The police arranged for the equipment to be escorted through the streets at high speed so that it could be flown out to Yugoslavia as quickly as possible. Everyone in Ljubljana was magnificent; kind and generous people. The women worked all night making Union Jacks to drape over the caskets, and a special burial site was earmarked if it was needed.

The relatives, however, wanted their loved ones sent back to the UK, and I managed to arrange for the RAF to provide aircraft to fly the bodies back to Britain.

Later, as thanks for the unstinting help of the people of Ljubljana, the Thomson Organisation presented scholarships for Yugoslav plastic surgery students to spend six months at a time in London hospitals to help further their training. The organisation also paid for the burns unit in the town to be re-equipped with modern facilities.

An inquiry into the crash blamed 'pilot error' and said that the aircraft altimeter had been incorrectly set for the airfield, which was 980 feet above sea level.

The crash caused further internal rumblings at Thomson Organisation, and more problems for **Gordon Brunton.**

Some of my board colleagues said the crash was terrible for the image of Thomson, and added that we should not be in the airline business. I agreed that it was dreadful but pointed out that there was much more likelihood of people being killed in a road accident than in an aircraft.

The backlash subsided and managers and staff prepared themselves for the introduction of the airline's first jetliner. Among those looking forward to the arrival of the Boeing 737 was 22-year-old female Cabin Crew **Jacky Clayton***, who joined the company in July 1966.*

I was interviewed by Elizabeth Harrison, who was the Chief Stewardess at the time. I remember going home to my parents in Cambridge and telling them about the interview when the 'phone rang. It was Elizabeth offering me the job.

Jacky Clayton joined the airline in July 1966, and within days was flying as number four stewardess.

The qualifications for the job included weight proportional to height; you should also not be any shorter than five feet four inches, and you had to be neat in appearance. You also had to swim. If you had a first aid qualification or a language, that was a real bonus. The Chief Stewardess was exceptionally well spoken, and the bigger the plum in your mouth the more chance you had of getting into the airline.

I started at Britannia within a few days. There were three of us who joined at the same time and it was considered rather unusual to be employed midway through the season, which in those days ran from April to October. Normally all training, both safety and cabin service, took between seven and ten days. However, we had one day's safety and emergency training under the control of Mike Forster, who was the Chief Flight Engineer. In the training session we had to learn and understand all about the emergency equipment and drills, and how to get passengers out of an aircraft in a hurry. At the end of the day we took a written examination and if Mike Forster was satisfied that we had met thecompany's and Civil Aviation Authority's standard requirements, we were ready to start our in-flight training.

I flew with Britannia for the first time two days later. The Britannia had a flight deck crew of three, and four Cabin Crew, ranked one, two, three and four. My early flights were usually as a number four stewardess and sometimes as a number three. The first duties as a number four stewardess consisted of packing the duty free goods into metal bar boxes, then collecting the passengers from the terminal and leading them out to the aircraft. We also had to lead them to the terminal when the aircraft landed.

One of my main duties in-flight was to help serve the food, usually a cold meal on the way out and a cottage pie on the way back. The passengers used to love it; the smell of the cottage pies heating in the ovens was always a source of pleasure to them. The aircraft had two galleys, one at the front and one midway to the rear. I loved the Bristol Britannia, although it was a little noisy. I had flown a lot before joining the airline, as my father was in

Jacky Clayton pictured at her retirement party with Bob Parker-Eaton (left) and Derek Davison.

the Foreign Service and we had been on flights to the Far East and Australia. But to those Stewardesses flying for the first time, it could be a problem; some suffered quite badly from airsickness. I remember coming back from a holiday flight at the beginning of the summer season and, as the aircraft was empty, Derek Davison, the pilot that day, had planned to use the time for flight crew training. He carried out a series of 'circuits and bumps', and those of us strapped in at the back were all feeling pretty dreadful.

Details of the ubiquitous cottage pie were highlighted by Britannia's Catering Manager, **David Douglas***, who found himself heavily quoted in the* Reading Evening Post [3] *in September 1967. The airline, he said, prepared 347,520 meals during the year, of which 176,500 were 'full meals'. During the peak times, Britannia used 12,000 bread rolls a week; around 1800 pints of milk a month; and 200,000 little sachets of salt and pepper. Outward bound menus were always chicken dishes, while return flights were 'typical English dishes' of beef, cottage pie or steak and kidney pie.*

We often get the comment, 'We have had a wonderful holiday and what we need to finish it off beautifully is a typical English meal.' So we give it to them.

Training for the arrival of the 737 had progressed apace and the first aircraft was due, after some slight setbacks, for delivery to Luton in July 1968, flown by Derek Davison and Don Tanton. Other pilots did not get their initial training at the Boeing plant in Seattle but in a darkened classroom at Luton. They were taking part in a 120-hour training course on a simple cockpit procedures trainer, developed by Britannia's engineers, who had built a mock-up of the aircraft's controls. It was soon known throughout Britannia as the 'cardboard bomber'. **Alan Hamilton,** *writing in the* Luton Evening Post, [4] *explained.*

The mock-up includes diagrams of every dial and switch in the complex cockpit. In addition, the pilots see 1500 colour slides of the control gear and everything in the 'plane that works. They are questioned closely on every one.

Known as the 'cardboard bomber', a mock-up of the 737 cockpit was built for pilot training at Luton.

All the pilots are fully experienced in the airline's Britannia turbo-prop fleet but the Boeing is new and different – so it's back to school.

Leading the course has been Mike Forster and Flight Engineer Rusi Parakh, an ex Air India man, both of whom have spent five weeks at the Seattle factory learning from Boeing engineers. When the first aircraft is delivered in July, the crews will still face hours of instruction in the air before they will be allowed to take passengers.

Before the arrival of the jets **John Sauvage** *was getting to know the twists and turns of his new company.*

You have to remember that when Thomson took over, the strategy of the airline had to change. It had to be part of the Thomson Organisation, which meant that many more resources were involved. The objectives had to change; Thomson was not interested in running a small group. Everything they did had to be big.

There was certainly a feeling in the early days from some in the airline that they did not want too much involvement with Thomson; they wanted the money, but not necessarily the involvement. That went on for quite a few months before it gradually began to change and they realised the sense of involvement with Thomson. I think it's fairly typical of most acquisitions; nobody really wants a new master. Once we got over that hurdle, matters developed very well indeed.

And for Britannia executives and staff, the best noise of the year was the gentle squeal of tyres on tarmac as the airline took delivery of Boeing 737 G-AVRL, which arrived from Seattle on 8 July 1968 under the careful control of Derek Davison with Don Tanton in the right-hand seat. Britannia became one of the first six airlines in the world to receive the 117-seat aircraft, which was destined to become the backbone of

Getting all the pieces together – a Britannia Airways jigsaw.

airlines across the globe. **Derek Davison** *told the press after touchdown:*

This is a wonderful 'plane. It's the most economical short-haul 'plane per passenger mile in the world, as far as we are concerned.

Bob Muckleston *was among the small Britannia team who went to Seattle to collect the 737.*

ABOVE Cabin Crew at work shortly after the introduction of the 737.

RIGHT A Boeing 737 of Britannia Airways in its late 1960s livery, which was changed in the early 1970s… to the striking red, white and blue livery.

Boeing did not believe we could do the flight back with only one stop at Goose Bay but we had done our sums and knew we could. The aircraft was stripped of all internal furnishings and we were supplied with just enough seats for our com-

plement. We sat for most of the journey on the brand new carpet playing cards and eating sandwiches and fruit supplied by Boeing. It was a wonderful experience, which was to be repeated many, many times as our fleet of Boeings grew.

The 737 arrival coincided with controversial plans by Luton Borough Council to develop the airport, which brought about predictable complaints from residents and equally predictable support from those likely to benefit.

Britannia's C-shift engineers take a break shortly after the Boeing 737 arrived in service. They are (left to right): Ernie Brooks, Jock Robertson, Terry Searles, Joe Chamberlin, John Weedon, Jim Cushion and Billy Bowden.

Into the furore Britannia injected vitally needed training flights for the 737, which caused a fresh round of complaints. The 'repetitive circuit' flights were made using noise abatement procedures. In a statement, **Derek Davison** *dampened concern.*

We are going to great expense and inconvenience to comply with these noise abatement procedures. It doubles the time between take-off and landing and in turn doubles the amount of flying time.

Three-quarters of our training is being carried out at other airports and all our training at Luton will be carried out in daytime. We are doing everything in our power to alleviate the situation at Luton but nevertheless we must have some training facilities at our base airport.

Love it or hate it, the Boeing 737 had arrived.

1 *Britannia's Management.* Published by *Flight International,* 1 June 1967.
2 *Langton quits Sky Tours.* Published by *Travel Trade Gazette,* 20 January 1967.
3 *You can't stop the plane at a corner shop,* by David Seymour. Published by the *Reading Evening Post,* 14 September 1967.
4 *Twelve pilots train to fly Luton's first jets,* by Alan Hamilton. Published by *Luton Evening Post,* 15 April 1968.

6. Turbulence

THE STATE-OF-THE-ART BOEING 737 that joined the Britannia fleet at Luton received plaudits from aircrew, cabin staff, passengers and press alike. Items that are taken for granted today were hailed as 'new concepts in flight luxury', including strip lighting, controlled fresh air boosters, reading lights, call buttons, seats with plenty of leg room and much more. Between them, Thomson and Britannia were showing the way in inclusive tour flights but the independent airlines were not all riding the crest of a wave and they all suffered the vagaries of indecisive government rulings on travel.

*In late 1968 British Eagle, the country's second biggest airline, collapsed with debts of around £7 million. A series of major financial blows had struck the company, which had been formed from virtually nothing after flying into Berlin during the 1948–49 blockade. The doyen of aviation journalists, **Arthur Reed**, wrote in* The Times[1]*:*

The Edwards Committee, currently looking into the future of all commercial aviation in Britain, is expected when it reports next spring to recommend wholesale rationalisation of the independents. By his decision to cease trading with British Eagle International Airways and British Eagle Aviation, his scheduled and chartered airlines, Harold Bamberg, Eagle's Chairman, proves that life for the independents was very tough – even before Edwards.

*Only weeks earlier **Lord Thomson** had attacked government regulations which kept holiday prices unnecessarily and artificially high as a deliberate policy. Speaking at a dinner in Budva, Yugoslavia, he said:*

The only real effect of these regulations is to make life difficult for everybody and to create additional complications and costs in administration.

The far-sighted Eric Atkinson who saw a business opportunity for 'positioning' aircrew and Cabin Crew.

But Britannia and Thomson continued to battle through the difficult times and by November 1968 the airline had seven Britannias and two 737s, whose capacity had been increased from 117 to 124 seats.

*A problem for all airlines was 'positioning' aircrew and cabin staff at different airports around the country. A far-sighted Britannia pilot, Captain Eric Atkinson, came up with an answer. The story is taken up by **Ian Garrett**, Managing Director of Hallmark Executive Travel Services, which has its head office in Luton.*

Eric Atkinson obviously saw a business opportunity looming and in 1968 with a friend of his, John Barnett, formed Hallmark, which

initially consisted of two or three cars and which was operated from a room at the back of John's television shop in Hemel Hempstead.

Initially they had no involvement with Britannia. They started with Dan Air and did some work for Cosmos before picking up business with Court Line.

By 1969 the groundwork put in by **John Sauvage** *in clinching Ministry of Defence trooping contracts had paid off, and a new and financially rewarding business was developed in moving soldiers, airmen and sailors to Germany.*

We were starting to expand in all areas by the early 1970s and it was part of the strategy to acquire business from a variety of different areas. Many charter flights were made for companies outside Thomson.

Not only that, the maintenance base at Britannia was by now looking after quite a lot of other people's aeroplanes, and doing a very good job indeed.

The trooping contract was helped along by **Bob Parker-Eaton***, who was later to join Britannia Airways but at the time was a Wing Commander working at the Ministry of Defence (MoD), managing all the civil air contracts as part of his service with the Royal Air Force.*

While I was with the MoD, British United Airways (BUA) gave notice to quit the Germany trooping contract, partly because we wanted rearward facing seats, which they found counterproductive, partly because they were not getting enough money and partly because the time band for the operation was crippling for them. The military would not fly before 10am and had to be back by 6pm.

I managed to get round the rearward facing seats problem, I got more money for British United, but the Army would not budge over these time bands and eventually we had to accept BUA's notice to quit.

I then had to find a replacement for this major contract. I went round all the airlines in Britain to try and find people who would take it on. Most of them could, in fact, but Britannia was the most likely prospect. They had just bought the Boeing 737 and had spare capacity the following summer when we needed it. I flew across to Germany with them because one of the things I was demanding was that Britannia turned the 737 round in 30 minutes in Germany and also accepted a very tight passenger reporting time in this country.

The 737 was replacing the BAC One-Eleven of BUA and the 30-minute turnaround time was easily achieved. The contract was agreed and Britannia started regular flights to five destinations in Germany – from Dusseldorf and Wildenrath in the west, and along 'the corridor' through the Russian zone to Berlin (Gatow) in the east. The contract was retained by Britannia for the next 25 years.

The number of passengers flying with Britannia continued to increase in the early 1970s. A fairly regular customer was Lord Thomson himself, who would 'phone **John Sauvage** *in advance to let him know he was travelling with the airline.*

He would turn up at Luton in a dark suit, wearing his normal pebble glasses and carrying two or three detective novels under his arm. He would fly down to one of the holiday destinations, spend a week down there walking around in his suit and then fly back. He never bought any leisure clothes and seemed quite happy to go everywhere in a suit.

Thomson, Horizon and Clarksons were among the top five operators, capturing some 50 per cent of the market between them, but the competition was 'brutal and savage', according to **Gordon Brunton.**

The Geoff Parkins hangar at Luton is big enough to take 1,300 double-decker London buses stacked from floor to ceiling. The hangar was named after one of the airline's technical directors.

We at Thomson Travel did not have our management right. I worked on the assumption that a manager was a manager was a manager, and after a lot of looking around for a Managing Director for Thomson Travel, I brought in Bryan Llewellyn, who was Marketing Director of Thomson Regional Newspapers, and a great deal of the success of our operation is subscribed to him. He knew nothing about the travel business but was an extremely able marketing man. He took over the whole thing and transformed it, and he brought in a great number of bright young men who were able to help with the success.

Meanwhile, Clarksons had decided to make some dramatic cuts in their rates, which were causing severe damage to our market share. The company was owned by Hambros Bank and I went and saw them to discuss the matter. I told them I thought this cut-throat operation was quite stupid and that no one would make any progress if it continued. They told me that their view was, and the advice they had been given was, that Thomson would not be able to stand the heat of the kitchen and they would be able to see us out.

I said we were not without resources and it would certainly not happen that way. Normally everybody put their holiday prices out at about the same time but on this occasion we waited until Clarksons had produced their brochures – and then we undercut them by ten per cent. We effectively destroyed them in one blow.

Aggressive marketing and 'head to head' competition urged by Bryan Llewellyn saw Clarksons and others lose out to Thomson Holidays, which from the early 1970s onwards dramatically increased its market share. And the airline itself was picking up the extra business and expanding its fleet. The Britannias were phased out in 1970 and 1971 as the 737s took on the extra work, and in February 1971 a leased Boeing 707 was added to the fleet; another 707 was added in 1972 and they were both used for long-haul 'affinity group charters'. The first, G-AYSI, was leased from World Airlines and arrived at Luton in February 1971, when it was given a revised livery in Britannia's new hangar. In the inaugural flight to Tenerife, the jetliner was flown by **Roy McDougall**, *who in December that year was involved in a 'longest day' flight in the 707.*

It was December 16 when the 'phone rang in my office and I was told that a 707 flight would be delayed for 14 hours because a spare part for the autopilot had not arrived from Seattle and the pilot, Don Tanton, had decided he did not want to fly without an autopilot. My instant reply was to inform Don that he had an autopilot, a human one, myself.

I drove the 15 minutes to my home, changed into my blue and gold uniform and left a note, 'Off to Los Angeles, back tomorrow afternoon'. It would not be that straightforward.

We took off on schedule and headed for Keflavik, our refuelling stop prior to crossing the North Atlantic, Canada and into California before landing at LA Airport. As per plan – well, not quite. As we approached the Scottish border, the number one hostess entered the flight deck to inform me that a passenger was dying and we should land soonest. That would be Manchester. Don explains to air-traffic control and we are soon heading back to Manchester Airport. We ask Manchester to arrange for an ambulance to meet us at the rear steps and I pick up the PA to inform the passengers. We also call base and put them in the picture.

Approaching Manchester, flaps half down, speed reduced and on final approach and the number one hostess appears with a strange-looking fellow in leather, with long hair and a ring in his ear, who announces that he is a doctor and that the patient was epileptic and would survive the journey. I order Don to overshoot and head again for Keflavik.

As we approach Greenland, the landing weather report gives reducing visibility with snow falling. As we are running late, with deteriorating weather, a decision was taken to keep the passengers on board while refuelling. This is never popular. The aircraft was given the lightest cabin clean, the toilets were cleaned and we were away.

ABOVE The sleek looking Boeing 707 jetliners were introduced for a short while in the 1970s.

LEFT Flight crew, led by Captain Roy McDougall, and Cabin Crew line up outside the Boeing 707 used in 1971 for the inaugural flight to Tenerife.

About a third through the take-off Don pulls back all throttles and says visibility is too poor for a take-off. I suggest we go back to the take-off point and review the situation. Agreed we should try again. This time we pass V1, no stopping now, V2 and Don eases our giant into the air – 178 passengers, ten crew and one human autopilot. On reaching cruising altitude, Don calls me to the Captain's seat to perform my duties of hand-flying our Boeing 707. It had already been a long day and was becoming longer. How long, I was to find out after landing in LA.

The spare for the autopilot had failed to be diverted and was now in Luton. Charming! So my services would still be required. I should have had five hours' sleep on the ground but before leaving Luton I had had a wisdom tooth removed and my jaw was beginning to swell. So in the early hours I had to find a doctor, explain the situation and get an injection.

Eventually the relief crew arrive. I explain things to the new pilot, Jim Watret. We board the passengers and away we go for a non-stop flight back to Luton. This takes ten hours and 20 minutes. My total airborne time was 22 hours and 35 minutes, five hours on the ground at LA, one in Keflavik, plus the three prior to take-off at Luton. I think I earned my crust that day.

I slept for a few hours at home before going to a dinner date with friends where, sadly, I fell asleep over coffee and had to be taken home.

The Boeing 707s had a short career with Britannia before being disposed of in 1973. A major political row had blown up over claims by scheduled UK airlines that the 'affinity' flights, where passengers had to belong to a so-called club, were undercutting their business. Britannia's Chairman, by then Sir Miles Thomas, had taken a verbal beating over the operations and eventually it was decided that the North Atlantic flights would be scrapped. Such protectionism for scheduled airlines was rampant.

The early 1970s saw an explosion in economic problems, all exacerbated by the Arab–Israeli war, during which oil supplies were cut to the West, and the Organisation of Petroleum Exporting Countries (OPEC) increased prices, adding to the woes of the airlines, which faced massive increases in bills for aviation fuel.

On top of all that, the financial shemozzle that hit parts of the travel industry became worse and in order to protect its charter business Court Line bought 85 per cent of the troubled holiday company Clarksons. In August 1974 the whole Court Line holiday and shipping complex came crashing down, leaving passengers stranded and holidays scrapped or lost.

Margaret Eagleton from Luton (left) and Sue Lloyd from Potters Bar, Hertfordshire, model Britannia Airways' new Cabin Crew uniform at Luton Airport.

The collapse took few prisoners, and companies and individuals around the country and in holiday spots around Europe went down with Court Line. In Luton, for instance, Hallmark found itself in big trouble. **Ian Garrett** *explains:*

Hallmark was fairly committed to Court Line at that time to the point that it had moved over to Luton and worked from a little yard attached to the back of a dairy where they had a 'Portakabin', a few cars and a minibus.

When Court Line failed, the company was left with a fleet of vehicles and almost no work. Hallmark circularised the airlines explaining that we had a fleet and plenty of experience. Someone at Britannia responded to the circular and sent a crew roster round and asked if we could price it. We looked at it and realised it was considerably more than we were used to, or to be honest could cope with, but we priced it anyway and sent it back. They showed an interest and one or two meetings were held and in the end they moved the contract to us and gave us six months to make sure that the bulk of it was being handled by our own vehicles rather than subcontracting.

It was a nationwide contract and we had to set about opening up branches around the country, which explains our national operation today. We started with Britannia in 1974 and have been with them ever since.

Two weeks prior to the Court Line collapse, a new face had arrived at Britannia. **Bob Parker-Eaton** *had left the RAF to join the Luton-based airline.*

I was on a transport course at Leeds University when I received a telephone call from Managing Director John Sauvage saying he had a problem with a post that needed filling in the airline. He said he was prepared to match my career prospects in the RAF and he wanted to know if I was interested.

I had three young children and needed another career, but not immediately. I was due to be promoted to the post of Deputy Director at the MoD. I had to weigh things up but I realised that I was unlikely to get another opportunity like this; I would not have wanted to work for most of the other airlines in this country but I was very interested in Britannia, which was still small but was growing fast. And so I accepted the post to create a new customer services division in the now fast-growing airline.

In early 1974 Britannia took delivery of the first of its advanced Boeing 737-200 series, with the so-called 'wide body interior look'. **Ray Hankin**, *writing in* TravelNews,[2] *had a look at the new jetliners.*

The advanced model 737 – Britannia is the first European user – looks for all the world like others of the same ilk but has two big advantages. The great plus-factor on the operating side, compared with the 11 already in Britannia service, it has an additional 300 miles range (for 1650 miles total) when flying out of Luton.

And from the 'good neighbour' point of view its 'hushed' turbofan engines mean a significant reduction in ground noise level, which is to be rewarded by the advanced 737 being included in Luton's night jet movement bonus for 'quiet' aircraft. Britannia intends eventually to refit its existing 737s with 'hush' kits but at a cost of £80,000 per aircraft the programme will not be completed until 1979.

*As the dust eventually settled on the Court Line debacle, Thomson began a recovery programme and by August 1974 was able to announce that it was putting 550,000 holidays on the market in the summer of 1975. Prices were up some 15 per cent, blamed largely on fuel prices and the effects of fluctuating exchange rates. Thomson Holidays' then Managing Director, **Francis Higgins**, told the press[3]:*

No immediate increase in capacity was planned as a result of the Court Line failure. The grounding of the Court fleet of 11 jets had brought supply and demand into a much closer balance.

*In a move to use their fleet fully, Britannia wet leased two 737s to Yemen Airways and two more for winter lease to Transavia Holland. Both deals were largely organised by **Bob Muckleston**. On the Yemen operation, he dealt with government ministers who were keen to shut down their airline – consisting of two old DC-8 freighters and two DC-9s – and hand the business over to a Saudi airline. After meetings with Yemen government ministers in London and the Yemen, he told the Britannia board that two 737s were required for the airline, whose main business was taking workers to Saudi Arabia.*

The return was good if we could handle the environment and could get the right deal. There was an anti reaction from the aircrew and maintenance side. The aircrew did not want to be posted to the middle of nowhere and the maintenance team did not want to support an aircraft in what was something of a hostile environment. However, our situation was grave if we could not find work for our two spare aircraft. We put together a spares pack and sent down two engineers together with some three crews. Initially the crews were sent there for a month and then rotated but the working environment was hard and if someone caught a cold it soon developed in the heat and dust into a major infection, requiring the crew member to be sent home.

One of Britannia's Boeing 737s in Yemen Airways livery.

By 1975 Britannia operated a total of 14 Boeing 737s and carried two million passengers.

All this business worried the scheduled operators, particularly British Airways (BA), formed by the merger of British European Airways and British Overseas Airways Corporation, and their executives moaned to the government about a variety of matters, including the so-called 'Wanderer' flights which they said were a 'misuse of the Britannia licence', because they used vouchers as well as cash, and most likely because they were offering packages at £59, as against BA's cheapest flight to Athens which was £125.

Rubbing salt into the wound, Britannia called its in-flight magazine at the time 'Wanderer', and in one issue,[4] which featured TV holiday commentator Judith Chalmers, it couldn't resist a certain amount of back-slapping.

Britannia's in-flight magazine, Wanderer, could not resist a certain amount of back-slapping when it detailed the airline's record on reliability, service and comfort.

You may not be aware of it but you are flying with Britain's leading holiday airline, and that's no idle boast. Britannia Airways carried more holidaymakers last year and flew more passenger miles than any other holiday airline in the country – and this year it looks like being top of the league again.

But sheer size isn't everything – reliability, service and comfort are equally important, and Britannia scores here too.

After detailing the advantages of the new 737-200s, the article touches on the 'crisp cool navy uniforms' which had been recently introduced for female Cabin Crew.

The new uniforms were designed by one of the airline's Senior Training Stewardesses, Herdis King, and are based on the mix-and-match concept which gives the girls a wide choice of wardrobe. Herdis researched the uniform over a period of four months, gaining valuable experience from the girls themselves. 'Simplicity' she said was the key to the design. It was vitally important because one must have a uniform which adapts to all shapes and sizes and still looks smart.

1 *Threat to Independents*, by Arthur Reed. Published by *The Times*, 7 November 1968.
2 *Britannia takes a new look but keeps it quiet*, by Ray Hankin. Published by *TravelNews*, 14 February 1974.
3 *15pc on tour firm's holidays*, by David Green. Published by *Manchester Daily Telegraph*, 29 August 1974.
4 *The Britannia Log*. Published in *Wanderer* by Britannia Airways, 1974/75.

7. The orange factor

FOURTEEN YEARS AFTER FLYING THE first Constellation airliner into the quiet acres of Luton Airport, Captain Derek Davison found himself with a new job at Britannia Airways –

as the company's Managing Director.

He was appointed in 1976 when John Sauvage took over as head of Thomson Travel and he rapidly set about acquiring more 737 jetliners to handle the extra business now flowing the airline's way. The upturn followed the OPEC crisis three years earlier and other national economic woes, which had hit the airline hard. Not only had these stripped more than 20 per cent from the anticipated summer holiday inclusive tours but they had also badly damaged the just-launched winter holiday programme that had been initiated by Bryan Llewellyn. The result was that Britannia managed to lease three of the 737s to the Dutch airline Transavia, which at least eased the financial problems.

The last of the 737s was back from Transavia by 1975, an expensive but vital Boeing 737 simulator was bought by Britannia a year later, and the airline set about getting on with the business of aviation.

In June 1977, six months after the appointment of Derek Davison, a new staff member arrived to help with the hustle and bustle of the Managing Director's life. **Anthea Billington** *took on the interesting and sometimes difficult role of secretary to the Managing Director, a job she still held as Britannia celebrated its 40th anniversary.*

I had worked in London for more than ten years but the commuting had become too much and I was looking for a job in Luton. I applied for the job at Britannia and found myself working for Derek Davison. He was not the easiest of men to work for – very demanding but very fair. He was of the old school and you would certainly not have called him Derek – he was always Mr Davison. Years later one of his successors instigated a system where everybody was called by their first name and that still applies in the airline today.

There were no women pilots in the airline when I joined and Derek Davison found women secretaries a necessary evil; I think if he could have done without them, he would. The appointment of women into the company did not figure high on the list of his priorities.

He still did a great deal of flying, usually the trooping flights because they were fairly quick and he could be back in the office within a relatively short time. He used to keep his uniform in the office so that he could change before going out to the aircraft. There was still a strong family feeling about the airline at the time; it was a much smaller entity; most people knew each other. The staff numbers were still quite small, hundreds rather than thousands, and Luton was the main hub, rather than today when most flights are from Manchester or Gatwick, even though Luton is still the headquarters.

It also had, and still has, a large number of families who are all connected with the airline in some way. It is the sort of industry that you either hate immediately or you enjoy and want to stay for life. Britannia is a very good company to work for and people who have left often come back again.

One of those to rejoin the company in 1974 had been **Bernard Newton.**

I rejoined as a Duty Engineer. Having worked for Euravia and Britannia previously from 1962 to 1964, it was attractive for me to come back to a company and people that I knew. I came from Donaldson Airlines at Gatwick, where I was a Licensed Aircraft Engineer on the Boeing 707. I gained my 737 licence at Luton and as I was still living in the Gatwick area and commuting to Luton, I welcomed the opportunity given to me by Geoff Parkins, the then Technical Director (after whom Hangar 61 was officially named in March 1990 by the Minister for Aviation) to set up a base at Gatwick to look after the airline's three 737 aircraft based there. I was a one-man band; I didn't have a vehicle or spares but I had enthusiasm and determination that Gatwick would be a great success. I started from scratch at Gatwick in 1976 and eventually got a vehicle, a few manuals and spares. I started to set what I considered to be the Britannia standards, i.e. the cleanliness of the aircraft and the minimum deferred defects. I used to be on 24-hour call, seven days a week. I relished the responsibility and knew that when the 'phone rang I had to go and 'fix' the problem, whether it was engine, airframe, avionics or radio. As I had all the required approvals on the 737s I was sometimes called out as many as three times in one night. I loved it, just loved it.

There were also problems to be solved for **Jacky Clayton**, *who had been flying as Cabin Crew on Boeing 737s from the time they were introduced.*

When I first started flying the 737 I was absolutely terrified. It was the unknown, I think, and the fact that we had a lot less time to do the work. In the old Britannia aircraft we were doing Luton–Palma in three hours and we had ample

Despite taking over as Managing Director Derek Davison (pictured left)
still did a great deal of flying.

time to provide the food, give a good drinks service and provide duty free goods. There was even time to talk to the passengers.

The 737 did the same flight in two hours. With four cabin staff, and with everything laid out in advance, we could just about complete the service but if we were busy on duty free sales it was difficult. Often we only just had time to put the stuff back in the bar boxes before we landed. The turnaround time abroad was 45 minutes and we had to dress the cabin – that involved taking all the passenger junk out of the pockets at the back of each seat, including apple cores, rubbish and often gooey stuff that had been crammed in there, and making sure that the sick bag, duty free booklet and, most importantly, flight safety leaflet was in there.

We used to wear turquoise crimplene dresses which came to just below the knee (regulation length) and which were not very useful for the work involved. One or two of us would be working in the galley when the aircraft was on the ground, preparing the meals for the flight. We would stand there with steaming ovens either side and sweat running down our faces, fronts and backs. In hot countries in July there was all the extra heat from the ground.

The Cabin Crew also had to deal with a variety of passenger health problems, including heart attacks, fainting and hyperventilating.

We were trained to help passengers who had fainted by putting their head between their legs, and treat hyperventilation by asking the person to breathe in and out of a paper bag. A lot of people felt quite anxious about flying, maybe because they were not in control of the situation – at least that's one theory we had.

After eight years' flying, **Jacky Clayton** *was made Deputy Chief Stewardess and a few months later she was made Chief Stewardess.*

When I took over I was in charge of some 150 cabin staff. When I left Britannia in 1985 I had 800 Cabin Crew and a management team of 36. Unfortunately it was impossible to know all 800! I absolutely loved the work and sometimes I used to sit back and think, 'We are the largest holiday charter company in the United Kingdom, and I am the Chief Stewardess. How did this happen?!'

When I started as Chief Stewardess, I was responsible for the on-line performance of the Cabin Crew and also responsible for hiring and firing. I did not

ABOVE The need to provide bigger aircraft with adequate range and good seat mile economics encouraged the decision in favour of the 767.

LEFT The substantial width of the Boeing 767 provided twin aisle convenience and eight abreast seating, which was a major attraction for Britannia.

feel very comfortable with the firing side but it had to be done – there were not many but it was nearly always for conduct that was prejudicial to the airline.

The Director's report and accounts for the 1970s were the very soul of brevity. In 1978, for instance, the report showed the Directors as Chairman Lord Thomas of Remenham (Sir Miles Thomas); Managing Director Derek Davison; and the other Directors as Bob Muckleston, Jimmy Little, Ray McDougall and Bob Parker-Eaton. It described the company's principal activity as 'the operation of a charter airline' and its finances showed a profit after taxation of £4,039,729, up from £2,589,231 the previous year.

By 1979 things were beginning to change in the country, and at Britannia Airways. The voters placed in power a Tory government led by Margaret Thatcher; in the airline, management was looking at projected business, which within five years would require new, bigger and more economic aircraft. During 1979 Britannia carried more than three million passengers on 18 Boeing 737s, with three more of the type on order.

On the technical side, matters were also increasing apace, explains **Bernard Newton.**

In 1979 Air Europe started their operation and approached Britannia to provide line maintenance at Gatwick. I was tasked to set up a proper line maintenance station which provided me with the opportunity to employ people, get them trained, set up the stores, the library, establish shift patterns and work ethics etc. We got Air Europe, who were flying 737s, off to a brilliant start and they didn't have their first technical delay for 12 weeks and that was only ten minutes.

Gatwick was thus the first line maintenance station away from Luton and this precedent was copied at other major UK airports. One of the men charged with looking at the wide range of possible new airliners was Project Manager **Bob Ginns**, *who had joined the airline in 1977.*

I used to be in technical sales at British Aerospace and by joining Britannia I was to some extent gamekeeper turned poacher. When I joined we just had 14 Boeing 737-200 airliners.

Looking at future fleets I produced a model which compared different aircraft types. This involved a great deal of input from colleagues and I was basically coordinating their comments and reports. I later became the focal point for the aircraft specification.

Concerns over high fuel prices, the need to provide bigger aircraft with an adequate range, good seat-mile economics, the long-term projections of Thomson Travel, the ability to operate from short runways and much more, eventually narrowed the choice of possible new aircraft to the Boeing 757-200, the Boeing 767 and the Airbus A310. Airline specialists, including George Berrisford, who was Britannia's Performance and Navigation Manager, flew to Seattle and the Airbus headquarters at Toulouse to check the facts and assumptions used in the evaluation. As **Bob Ginns** *points out:*

The aircraft specification really was a team effort. It involved lots of people in engineering, flight operations, cabin services, catering and other areas. We wanted to use the new aircraft properly by getting high utilisation out of them and being able to introduce a reasonable number of them in a short time.

After months of detailed planning and consideration, the decision was finally made to go for the Boeing 767 and on 1 January 1980, Managing Director Derek Davison submitted a recommendation to Gordon Brunton and the Thomson board for the purchase of two of the aircraft, with three more to follow. Approval was given but there was still plenty of work ahead for many people, as **Bob Ginns** *explains:*

We then started the engine competition. We also worked on the aircraft specification. In retrospect the choice of the aircraft, the Boeing 767-200 over the A310, and the choice of the GE CF6 engine over the Pratt and Whitney JT9 were absolutely correct.

Moving to the present day on aircraft deliveries, it has become my role to coordinate matters from a commercial perspective, also helping to ensure engineering are happy with the technical aspects of the delivery, the airworthiness of the aircraft and the paperwork, so that we can get the Federal Aviation Administration export certificate from the US and the Civil Aviation Authority certificate from the UK.

It is one of the fascinating things about working in aviation; no one person has all of the information or even most of the information – it is a lot of people working together. Mind you, the number of people now working in the airline has increased dramatically over the years

This picture is of a skin change on the aft-fuselage of a Boeing 737-200 in the mid-eighties. The engineers are Tony Barber (left) and Tony Berti (right).

A passenger eye view from a 757 on final approach to Palma.

and we don't all know each other as well as we did when it was smaller. When I joined the company, for instance, the performance department had three people; now it has around 15. Personnel had three and now has 33, and several departments did not even exist. It felt very much a family, and everybody could talk to each other.

When I arrived, the Technical Director was Jimmy Little, who could be very direct and once said to me: 'I don't know what you are here for; I don't know why we need a Project Manager.'

About six months later we were about to sign an agreement to purchase another 737 and I noticed by chance that the escalation formula we had been given in the agreement to sign was different from the formula in the proposal, which we had accepted. I think it was an honest mistake by Boeing but it did involve $500,000. Once we had sorted the matter out Jimmy Little said to me: 'Perhaps you are some good, after all.'

Then I felt that I had become part of Britannia.

Britannia passengers in the early 1980s did not have to worry themselves about the problems of running the airline. On their flights to and from Palma, or Alicante, or Rome, or Rhodes, or Vienna, or any one of a wide variety of destinations, they could eat, drink, buy duty free – and wonder about the weight of an orange! In an article in the in-flight magazine of the airline[1] in early 1980, **Jack Moss,** *Manager of In-Flight Services, wrote:*

Weight is a limiting factor in these days of soaring oil prices. The cost of additional fuel to carry even a few kilos of catering equipment is prohibitively expensive. We calculated recently that if we were to add a large orange to the meal of every passenger, our fuel bill this year would be increased by no less than £50,000.

1 *Eating Aloft,* by Jack Moss. Published in *Britannia* magazine, spring 1980.

8. The battle to save the fleet

IN EVERY RESPECT THE ELEGANT new jetliner being built at Seattle by Boeing was the ideal addition to the Britannia fleet. The 767 was an entirely new aircraft, designed to make maximum use of the latest technology by providing fuel efficiency and twin-aisle passenger convenience.

The twin General Electric CF6-80A turbofans gave a reliable service, enabling a cruising speed of up to 600mph, with a range of up to 3700 miles and a capacity of up to 270 passengers.

Production of the aircraft started in 1978 with an order for 30 of the type for United Airlines. Britannia was the first airline in Europe to order the Boeing 767 – as it was 20 years earlier with the Boeing 737-200 – and again did so off the drawing board. The rivalry between Boeing, anxious for European orders, and Airbus, anxious to keep Boeing out, meant that Britannia was able to obtain an extremely attractive price.

In their book Boeing, Planemaker to the World,[1] *authors* **Robert Redding and Bill Yenne** *explain.*

The development of the 767 was an intensive effort aimed at refining the design to give maximum fuel performance, operational flexibility, low noise levels, advanced aircraft systems – including digital electronics – in the most advanced airliner deck and, finally, growth potential.

The 767's two-aisle passenger cabin follows the tradition established in the 747, which was the original wide-body jetliner.

But every airline has different views and needs and Britannia needed nearly 100 modifications to the final version that was delivered to Luton. That meant some tough decision-making for **Bob Ginns.**

We had to justify every item – either it paid for itself or we did not buy it. In theory we wanted to purchase the standard Boeing aeroplane: everything extra had to be justified by the bottom line. We certainly did not buy anything for purely cosmetic effects.

On the customer services side, **Bob Parker-Eaton** *was concerned that the 767 could provide all that was needed.*

Our major problem was that we knew nothing about wide-bodied aircraft. I flew and visited with a number of airlines to learn from their experience and to see how they could help us. We had to look at the aircraft and decide what we really needed for Britannia. My key man in many areas was Roger Weeks. He looked at areas like the galley, cargo loading, containers and so on. The 767 was too narrow to have the standard containers side by side, so Roger and I eventually came up with a system that used containers for the rear hold with a walkway alongside and which would permit both containerised and manual loading, and a large Boeing container for the front hold, which would hold both large items and any overflow from the rear. We were always looking for ways of speeding overseas turnarounds, and stowage under the floor was one way of ensuring that all the rubbish in the aircraft is dumped into a fireproof container which is then emptied and replaced at the home airport. It was also a good flight safety point because on a long flight you have rubbish bags blocking the doors of the aircraft as the only place the cabin crew can put them. By putting them through the hatch in the floor it meant they did not have to be offloaded abroad and there was more space for the Cabin Crew operating in the aircraft.

At the time, controversial decisions were also taken by Britannia to reduce the flight crew from three to two, and that meant a flight deck that was far too large. Again, **Bob Parker-Eaton** *and his team were able to turn that to the advantage of the airline.*

It always annoyed me over the years that some of the overhead lockers in aircraft were taken up with overnight bags and other items for the Cabin Crew, when they should have been available for passengers. I managed to get Boeing to design a cupboard to fill the space left by the smaller flight deck, for Cabin Crew stowage. Over the years that became a standard Boeing option.

Other changes included moving the toilets to the centre of the aircraft to avoid blocking the galley with waiting passengers, and water dispensers which the passengers could use to cut down the Cabin Crew time.

While they looked forward to the arrival of the 767, Britannia staff still had plenty of other matters to deal with at the start of the 1980s. A new operations centre was opened at Luton, the fleet size increased to 23 Boeing 737s, four million passengers were carried in 1981 – and a new cabin staff uniform was introduced. Jacky Clayton, Ann Rhodes, Bob Parker-Eaton and many others were involved in the new design, which had taken four years from planning to realisation. **Terri Eastaff,**

LEFT Several Britannia aircraft were named after great aviators, and in March 1981 a Boeing 737 – G-BGYL – was named after Jean Batten.

BELOW After the naming ceremony Jean Batten inspected the cockpit of 'her' aircraft assisted by First Officer Suzanne Eastbury.

writing in Offchocks,[2] *the newsletter of Britannia Airways cabin staff, said the hats would be made in Luton – the largest hat-producing region in Britain.*

A suit and coat were made by Ideal Clothiers in pure wool. As Ann was visiting the factory herself, the uniform was made to fit her. Ann wore the suit and coat on about 20 flights, taxiing here, there and everywhere between our bases to give it a good testing.

A company, Leslie Whitley, was called in as they specialised in blouse manufacture. Their representative agreed to design a material using red, white and blue in a lightweight polyester with special emphasis on washability. This was in the same style as originally agreed, long- or short-sleeved with a two colour choice – blue and white on red, or blue and red on white.

Apron, shoes – in navy calf leather with a small gold chain on the front – handbag, belt, cabin bags, brevet and gloves were all details. A new uniform for male Cabin Crew was also being planned. The new look was not confined to uniforms. There was a new red, white and blue livery for the fleet and changes to the aircraft interior. The logo was changed from Britannia Airways to Britannia.

Britannia's second 767, G-BKPW, Earl Mountbatten of Burma, *was highlighted in a special first day cover marking a celebration flight shortly after delivery to Luton.*

By the early 1980s, several Britannia aircraft were named after 'great Britons'. The names included James Watt, Sir Francis Drake, General James Wolfe, Sir Arthur Whitten Brown, Florence Nightingale, Sir Walter Raleigh, Sir Barnes Wallis *and* R.J. Mitchell *and, in March 1981,* Jean Batten, *an early record-breaking pioneer of long-distance flying. She attended the naming ceremony, which included a reception, lunch and a tour of Britannia's home. Later* **Jean Batten** *wrote to Bob Parker-Eaton.*

I would like once again to tell you how much I enjoyed the ceremony and reception, and how honoured I feel that a Britannia Airways 737 airliner now bears my name. I found the tour of your establishment most interesting and was really impressed by the obvious air of efficiency, the team spirit and general feeling of happiness and contentment at all levels which is, alas, all too rare nowadays.

By 1982 there were some major management changes within the company. Captain Dave Hopkins, who had joined the airline in 1967 and later became Chief Pilot,

RIGHT Managing Director Dave Hopkins (right) with Sir Frank Whittle, inventor of the jet engine, at a naming ceremony for a Britannia airliner.

BELOW There have been several other naming ceremonies at Britannia including a 767 which was christened Earl Mountbatten of Burma. *The ceremony was attended by Countess Mountbatten and her sons Philip and Timothy.*

was made a Director of Britannia in January that year, and **Derek Davison** *was appointed Chairman and Chief Executive. With two 767s on order, three more in the pipeline and 34 Boeing 737 airliners, he was ready for expansion when he ran into a little trouble with his masters at International Thomson.*

By this time Gordon Brunton had left International Thomson, which was a great shame. He had always been able to see the importance of Britannia and the support it gave to the tour operation. He knew that by putting the two together we had achieved the right result and always made a profit. He said to me on more than one occasion, 'When you have a winner you back it', referring to the provision of capital for aircraft acquisition. After his departure there was a certain difficulty at International Thomson in understanding how Britannia could perform so well and there developed an argument that it must be at the expense of tour operating.

The background to this was a change in Thomson Holidays over the years from having a real pride in the performance of its sister airline to one of envy in its profitability record, not helped by the introduction of a bonus scheme. In fact, Britannia's record reflected in essence the airline charter markets whilst Thomson Holidays' record reflected the more unpredictable and more difficult tour operating market. The new management at International Thomson was persuaded that the difference between the two financial performances was substantially due to capital for aircraft acquisition being used by Britannia on behalf of tour operators competing with Thomson Holidays. There had been some indication of this at a previous meeting with International Thomson and I got a very definite impression that whilst I was politely listened to on this subject, I was not believed.

After the meeting I felt a new face was desirable and I asked Dave Hopkins, who was then the Deputy MD, to prepare a presentation showing how each and every aircraft in the fleet was being used by Thomson Holidays; he produced a bar chart which showed that in summer every aircraft in the fleet except one at Glasgow had been used sometime by Thomson Holidays. It also showed that we simply could not accommodate the Thomson programme with fewer aircraft.

At the subsequent presentation to International Thomson I asked Dave to present the chart. They looked at each other and made it quite clear that they had not previously understood the situation. We had made some progress in changing previously closed minds.

FACING PAGE

A Boeing 767 for Britannia Airways under construction in Seattle.

Chairman Derek Davison (left) accepts the keys of a 767 from Boeing Chairman T. Wilson.

But there were more shocks ahead for **Derek Davison.**

It all came to a head when I was summoned to International Thomson's London HQ at Stratford Place for a meeting with the new President of International Thomson and two of his colleagues.

I had been warned that it was a serious meeting to discuss fleet reduction, so I took Peter Brown, Britannia's Financial Director, along with me. To my amazement, they wished to reduce the size of the 737 fleet by 17 aircraft. The meeting lasted two or three hours and in the end I was asked to agree the sale of three old 737s. I received a letter some three days later thanking me for being so understanding in agreeing to sell three aircraft.

Typical internal politics, I suppose, but it did leave me wondering about the future. However, we had won the battle if not the war and importantly, the top people at International Thomson realised how we were looking after shareholders' interests as well as providing good profits. Subsequently more aircraft and hangar capacity were approved.

The early 1980s saw some career changes for Bernard Newton.

Late 1982 also saw changes for **Bernard Newton**, *who was also being promoted.*

Geoff Parkins, the Technical Director who had asked me to go to Gatwick, died in 1982. At his funeral I renewed my acquaintance with Bill Buxton, who asked if I would be interested in returning to Luton as the Deputy Maintenance Manager, and after some consideration I agreed.

Bill Buxton had been brought in as a caretaker Technical Director until a new one could be appointed. **Bernard Newton** *continues:*

He set up a senior management structure of four people, two managers and two deputies, to determine his successor. He swapped us around in various management positions within engineering and maintenance over the next two years and I welcomed the opportunity to learn more about each department. The two years passed very quickly and then one Friday night I met Bill as I was walking through the hangar. We were both of the old school and turned out lights that were not needed, and so we met in the hangar with just enough light to see by, when he said: 'Oh, by the way you are going to be the next Technical Director.' I was somewhat surprised and extremely delighted but I had to keep this information to myself for three months and still work alongside my three colleagues.

In February 1984 the first Boeing 767 arrived at Luton after an almost trouble-free flight from Seattle with the delivery crew of Captains Dave Hopkins, Eric Turner and Nick Pennington. A fuel booster pump used as a backup system caused a problem on flight but the aircraft did not turn back and landed at Luton one minute early to a media welcome. The 767 – G-BKVZ – was named Sir Winston Churchill *and was followed by G-BKPW, which was named* Earl Mountbatten of Burma.

By the mid 1980s Britannia operated 27 Boeing 737s and four 767s and was carrying 4.3 million passengers. Among them were **Terry and Iris Barnes***, who started flying with Britannia in the mid 1970s.*

We usually travel to Palma twice a year and have always been with Thomson and Britannia. The early trips used to cost us £28 for nine days. It's changed a bit since those days but the Britannia service has always been good and we always feel well looked after. As far as we are concerned, once we have arrived at the airport and checked in our bags then the holiday begins. We don't have to worry about too much after that; there is always someone to help us.

Passengers Terry and Iris Barnes remember the days when holidays used to cost £28 for nine days.

Terry has been a photographer for many years and still has film of the early holidays in Spain.

It's all changed since then, with hotels and accommodation all over the place, and the aircraft have changed inside and out, but we still feel comfortable with Britannia. We must have done well over 50 trips with the airline – but we still don't get a discount!

Persuaded to return to the airline in 1985 as Cabin Services Manager was **Helen Butler***, who had taken a three-year break from Britannia to look after newly arrived twin boys. She had originally joined as Cabin Crew in 1974 and left as a Cabin Services Manager.*

Helen Butler joined as Cabin Crew in 1974, and was promoted to Cabin Services Manager in 1985.

My new job included specifying the onboard products and providing instructions for the onboard crew. I was no longer flying but I came back to the 767 aircraft, which were very good for the Cabin Crew – much more space to move around.

For years I was responsible for the work the crew did on board, the catering, including getting the food on the aircraft, the products we bought, marketing them, the in-flight entertainment and programmes. I had a staff of about 40 who were responsible for all in-flight services. A lot of people doing the job were ex-Cabin Crew, including me, as it was important to understand the workload involved and to make sure that it could work operationally. Even today, the General Manager In-Flight and Retail is ex-Cabin Crew. It is important to understand that the service you are specifying is deliverable.

By 1986 the new Managing Director was announced as former Chief Pilot and Operations Director Dave Hopkins and he worked closely with Derek Davison on the continued development of the airline. Britannia had already become involved in some scheduled services from Manchester and Gatwick to holiday spots including Tenerife, Las Palmas and Malaga but was still looking around for new possibilities, explains **Dave Hopkins.**

The Commercial Director Brian Christian and I came up with the idea of charter flights to Australia during the winter months. For years, flying Muslim pilgrims to Mecca for the annual Hadj had been useful winter business for Britannia but as the pilgrimage dates gradually moved forward we still had a problem with winter operations. Brian and I looked at the Australian possibility and pursued the idea of IT [inclusive tour] flights. It did not provide an awful lot of revenue but it was a way of keeping the aircraft occupied and of paying a few bills.

There was a certain reluctance in Thomson over the Australian flights because they felt that Britannia was very good at European operations but had little experience in long-haul. We got over that in the end and the charters continued for several years.

TOP Bob Parker-Eaton and his team spent time
looking at ways of improving the basic 767.

ABOVE A Britannia 767 ready for its passengers.

LEFT Wide-screen viewing and headsets for in-flight
passengers in the 1970s.

The changing face of Johnnie Walker. Onboard, tax free gifts were always in demand in the 1980s, including Johnnie Walker whisky at £5.75 a bottle. Britannia continues to offer a wide range of duty free products.

Travel with No.1

...nnie Walker, the world's No.1 Scotch whisky.

"We can't correct the past but we **might** change the future."
WIN LYOVARIN

KEEP WALKING

Johnnie Walker

Fiercely opposed by the scheduled competitors, Britannia's flights, the first regular charter operation to Australia, opened up that continent to major UK originating tourism and were the direct cause of a tumbling of scheduled economy fares.

With many airports still slow to develop fully the duty free facilities, onboard duty and tax free gifts were always popular in the 1980s. A quick reminder of prices in the past for the lucky Britannia passengers shows:

Johnnie Walker whisky – bottle	£5.75	Gin – half bottle	£1.85
Bacardi – half bottle	£1.85	Dunhill cigarettes – 200	£4.90
King Edward cigars – 25	£10.00	Chanel No 5 – 7ml	£11.95
Givenchy aftershave – 60ml	£3.50	Sheaffer pen and playing cards	£2.50
Pierre Cardin lighter	£16.50		

1 *Boeing, Planemaker to the World,* by Robert Redding and Bill Yenne. Published by Arms and Armour Press, London, 1983.
2 *The making of a new uniform,* by Terri Eastaff. Published in *Offchocks,* the newsletter of Britannia Airways cabin staff, December 1979.

9. Flight plan

FOR THE COUNTRY AND FOR THE travel industry, the late 1980s were proving testing times. By January 1988 Margaret Thatcher had become the longest continuously serving Prime Minister in the 20th century but the year was to see the first of a series of interest rate hikes and an admission by Chancellor Nigel Lawson that the economy was in decline. In the same year, Thomson paid £75 million for Horizon, cementing its dominance as the country's largest tour operator.

Author **Roger Bray**, *writing in* Flight to the Sun,[1] *details the background.*

This Horizon, of course, was not the company founded by Vladimir Raitz. It was the former Horizon Midland (floated off by Vladimir as a public company in 1972), rescued from the flames of the Court Line crash by a consortium led by Bruce Tanner. It had changed its name to Horizon Travel in 1979, when memories of the financial problems which had beset the original Horizon were dimmed. Its airline (Orion) was launched a year later. In 1987 it had acquired Wings from Rank and was itself bought soon afterwards by the brewers Bass for £94 million. Thomson, which carried around 3.5 million passengers a year, controlled some 30 per cent of the market. Horizon's one million represented ten per cent. Together they would be roughly double the size of their nearest rival, the International Leisure Group. Lord Young, the Trade Secretary, referred the takeover to the Monopolies and Mergers Commission, which gave its blessing the following January.

Britannia's Managing Director, **Dave Hopkins**, *found himself in the thick of the takeover problems shortly after moving into his new job.*

We had discussed the matter in advance with Thomson and our attitude was that it should not be done from the point of view of Britannia growing. We would rather grow organically than take someone over, which would mean inheriting some of their problems.

However, it went ahead and inevitably we did inherit some problems. It's hard to walk into another airline and say you are now part of us, but we had to do that with Orion and it took a lot of effort to go through the period of change and integration. One of the interesting sidelines was that we discovered that we had always overestimated how good they were and the deals they had. When we got in there and saw the other side, we realised we had given them a lot of credit they didn't deserve. The only exception we discovered was that the rates they had negotiated with their handling agents in Greece were better than ours.

They also had a number of minority interests in a variety of areas, including an airline in Spain. With three other groups also holding 25 per cent, it meant that no one was in charge. It taught me that if you are not controlling something, you have to have a very good reason for a minority share. We managed to offload our liability for the Spanish operation.

More work for the airline meant more pressure on staff, and Britannia Airways had become a UK and world leader in the study of the medical effects of flying on flight and Cabin Crew, largely through the work of **Dr Alan Roscoe,** *who joined the airline in 1983 as its Chief Medical Officer. After internationally acclaimed reports on pilot workload, he turned his attention to the effects of flying on Cabin Crew health and performance, particularly the so-called flight attendant 'burnout' syndrome. His report, presented at the 5th Annual International Aircraft Cabin Safety Symposium in Oakland, California, explained:*

Examination of the case histories of 100 (97 female) consecutive consultations for recurring minor illnesses – mainly upper respiratory tract infections – seen over the previous five years at Britannia Airways revealed that a disproportionate number had been flying for between four and six years at the time of consultation and, importantly, most had previously been quite healthy. This epidemiological evidence suggests that many of these individuals were suffering from the cumulative effects of flying – the flight attendant 'burnout' syndrome. Further support for this diagnosis was obtained on re-examining several of these patients, when almost two-thirds admitted to symptoms which included lethargy, forgetfulness, loss of concentration, recurring headaches and irritability; and, in some cases, to a lack of motivation to fly.

The stresses and strains of Cabin Crew are occasionally not helped by the antics of passengers. **Bob Parker-Eaton** *recalls a 737 flight out of Palma to Birmingham.*

It concerns a couple who were not married to each other but who sat next to each other on the flight. At some point during the flight they disappeared into a lavatory together but omitted to bolt the door. A little old lady waiting outside the lavatory realised that the couple were having sex. She was absolutely horrified by this and reported it to the Cabin Crew, and the Cabin Crew didn't know what to do, so the Number One went to the Captain and explained the problem.

The Captain was a man of action; he knew exactly what to do. He told his

On Air
VIDEO

PROGRAMME GUIDE
FOR FLIGHTS TO THE UK
January — March 1993

Britannia

ABOVE The ubiquitous Boeing 737s became the workhorse for Britannia and many other airlines around the world.

RIGHT Britannia's in-flight programme guide in the 1990s.

First Officer to go back and sort it out! By the time the First Officer headed back to the lavatory, the couple were in their seats and fast asleep with big smiles on their faces, and the First Officer didn't have the heart to do anything about it. The senior Cabin Crew member's post-flight report achieved a much wider circulation than normal.

And even tragedy can have a touch of comedy.

On a flight from Manchester a male passenger had a heart attack and unfortunately was dead by the time the aircraft had diverted to Bristol. The ambulance crew took the body off and our crew were explaining to the widow that they could not get their baggage off before the aircraft arrived at Palma, where it would be offloaded and flown back to the UK.

She was most upset. 'What do you mean, take it off? I have paid for this holiday and I am going to Palma,' she said. And that's exactly what she did.

Bearing in mind we carry some ten million passengers a year, there are very few deaths on board, and the crew and the airline do everything they can to ease the pain for the bereaved. There was, however, one occasion when the crew were surprised by a widow who was flying back from Spain with her husband's body in the hold. She was buying double quantities of duty free whisky and cigarettes and the crew pointed out the legal amount that she could take back into the UK. 'Oh,' she said, 'that's alright, there's always the entitlement for him in the hold.'

By January 1989 Orion's fleet was operated by Britannia Airways. By year end the fleet consisted of eight Boeing 767s and 32 Boeing 737s. The company had orders for eight 767s for delivery in 1990 through to 1993. During 1989, seven million passengers were carried. Some of the passengers were flown by the company's Managing Director, **Dave Hopkins**, *to and from their holiday destinations.*

Very few Managing Directors have the advantage of running the company and also being able to see what is going on in the real world – out on the line. I was able to arrive on the flight deck as the pilot, and largely people forgot that I was the Managing Director. I was able to fly the route and perceive much more of what was really happening along the way.

After all, I had been flying for 21 years and the crews were happy enough to see me in the left-hand seat. I think they soon forgot that I was the MD.

There were more management changes in 1989, with Dave Hopkins moving to Chairman and the arrival in November that year of **Roger Burnell***, who became the company's new Managing Director. He had previously been Managing Director at Thomson's Lunn Poly operation.*

I was the first Managing Director of Britannia not to have been a pilot. My immediate disadvantage was that I knew little about flying and so I decided to learn to fly, which is very convenient at Luton because Britannia has its own flying club on the airfield.

This meant that at the very least I knew what was going on from an operational point of view and I knew the terminology.

An early task was to take a good look at the business and I employed some external consultants to help with the process. What we discovered from this review was that although everyone in the airline thought Britannia provided the best customer services, and we were the best in the business, the reality was that it was no longer true.

A strategic review for the airline, titled Flight Plan *for the 1990s, was introduced by Managing Director Roger Burnell.*

In the 1980s several holiday airlines had been started up – Horizon started Orion, the International Leisure Group started Air Europe and Air 2000 had been formed. Thomson Holidays, as a tour operator, did most of its flying with Britannia but it also contracted the other airlines. We soon discovered that the quality score with airlines like Air 2000 was better than Britannia. On every Thomson holiday there is a questionnaire to fill in on the way back; it includes questions on the resort and the hotels, and there are about six questions about the flight.

From that we discovered there were airlines out there doing better than Britannia. We also looked at the aircraft. When the 737s were brought in some 20 years earlier they were way ahead of their time but by 1989, this was no longer the case. The Boeing 757 was now becoming the workhorse of the charter airlines in the UK; it was more efficient, more reliable and comfortable. We compared ourselves with Air 2000 and they had an all-757 fleet.

The situation was not all Britannia's fault. Within Thomson Holidays a view had evolved that getting their flying in 130-seater chunks was the ideal. Even the 767s exactly doubled that number of passengers and so you could effectively fit two chunks into one aircraft.

So we now had a situation where the service was not as good as it should have been and, related, the fleet was getting tired looking.

Finally, the costs of running the airline were too high. An example was the way the pilot workforce was employed. Because the base was at Luton, the pilots had been employed at Luton and that meant that 50 per cent of the pilots were based at Luton, although it only represented a small percentage of the flying. At least 55 per cent of the flying was out of Gatwick or Manchester, with the result that we had pilots in taxis being ferried around or in hotel beds. This resulted in a huge and expensive inefficiency.

The result of the strategic review was a plan, which was called 'Flight Plan for the 1990s'. **Roger Burnell** *describes some of its effects.*

This was a very public statement making it clear that there were going to be changes. We sent a video to every member of staff, which arrived on their doorstep, explaining what was going to happen, to show that we were serious about our plan.

The net result was that we had around 220 redundancies, and about 170 moves around the company. That doesn't really tell you the number of jobs that were actually lost. When I joined, the engineering department, for instance, was recruiting at a phenomenal rate so that they could maintain the ageing 737s. We called a halt to all that and explained that we were going to change the fleet.

We started to introduce Boeing 757s and started to lose some of the Boeing 737s. I think everybody in the company realised that the changes were overdue and I did not get a huge backlash from the staff or the unions.

The objective was that everyone was in place by the summer of 1991, with the pilots based at different airports. We also started a study of replacement aircraft for the 737s and after a lot of investigation, including looking at a possible Airbus A320, we made the decision to stick with 757s and 767s. By 1992 we had sold all the 737-300 series airliners that we had inherited from Orion and were looking to sell off the 737-200s.

Project Manager **Bob Ginns** *takes up the story.*

There was, and is, a lot of commonality between the 757 and the 767 in terms of components but more important was the flight-deck and crew commonality. People think that we are an all-Boeing airline but we are always looking at alternatives and we have to take what aircraft are around at the time. If, for instance, the Airbus A321 had been around in the early 1990s, that could have been the ideal choice.

Whatever the aircraft in the Britannia fleet, they worked hard for the airline, as Technical Director **Bernard Newton** *can testify.*

We were looking at flying some 4500 hours a year on the Boeing 737s, and perhaps 6000 hours a year with the 767. Certainly as the 737s got older they required a great deal of maintenance, but the 757 and 767 were more sophisticated and required a lot less maintenance. In fact, in 1993–94 when we rolled over the whole fleet and got rid of the last of the 737s, it halved overnight the maintenance requirements.

Keeping the airline flying was paramount and Managing Director Roger Burnell found himself with a problem in 1994 when strike action was threatened by Cabin Crew in a dispute over pay and conditions. **Anthea Billington** *was one of those asked to step into the breach.*

I went to East Midlands Airport to learn how to become a Cabin Crew member, together with people from throughout the company and some 100 or so staff from Lunn Poly.

It was Roger's plan, and he was determined to keep the aircraft flying. It went virtually to the wire before it was satisfactorily resolved without any industrial action.

On the ground, too, there was a determination to provide Britannia flight and Cabin Crews with the best comfort available as they were 'positioned' from airport to airport. **Ian Garrett** *of Hallmark explains:*

We work for several airlines but Britannia is our largest contract. They are fairly hard people – they know what they want, but as long as you give the attention and service they need, they are happy. We have built a good relationship over the years. The work has spread over the years; it was initially just crews but now it is also management travel and other work for the airline and Thomson Travel with overbookings or delays.

Our fleet has changed and now includes coaches. For a while we had minibuses and in the early days we had one where the engine was directly along-

side the driver. The top speed was 50mph and the vibration was terrible; driver and passengers would still be shaking when they got out.

As Britannia moved to larger aircraft and larger crews we were having to use four cars to move people about. Britannia suggested we look at coaches and initially we got an old second-hand Bedford, which was a bit of a heap. Once Britannia had decided that coaches would be the answer we decided to go for modern, efficient vehicles and high specification.

When we were selecting coaches we took Captain John Hough, the then British Air Line Pilots' Association (BALPA) representative, to the coach show at the NEC in Birmingham. John was a big man and when we were selecting seats we went to all the seat suppliers for John to help choose the one that suited best.

Nowadays the coaches have coffee machines, tables, toilets and video players, leather seats and ovens at the back. We have always gone for top of the range; we always tried for good-quality cars and when we got into coaches the same applied. The latest coaches we have are award-winners – and they cost around £350,000 each.

1 *Flight to the Sun. The Story of the Holiday Revolution,* by Roger Bray and Vladimir Raitz. Published by Continuum, London and New York, 2001.

10. Flying – with confidence

THE WAY TO MAKE MONEY WITH A charter airline is certainty, and it was with that basic thinking and determination that Britannia Airways set about confirming its role in life during the early and mid 1990s.

Managing Director **Roger Burnell** *had made sure that despite the country's economic problems, particularly the debacle of 'Black Wednesday' in September 1992 when Britain suspended its membership of the Exchange Rate Mechanism (ERM), the airline stuck to its plan and knew how its business should be run.*

We had to realise that Britannia was part of an integrated travel group. It had the idea that it was an independent airline, and it wasn't. The group at the time had some 18 scheduled licences, which we canned to concentrate solely on charter operations.

We then focused the need on serving Thomson tour operations and quite quickly we moved the percentage of flying for Thomson to over 90 per cent. The planning became much more of a dual activity, with both companies actively involved.

We set up the operation internally so it was in the interest of Thomson Holidays to fly the aircraft as intensively as possible; they got cheaper and cheaper seat rates the more they flew the aircraft. That meant we moved the aircraft utilisation up dramatically.

Certainty is the key, so that if you plan to fly a certain programme and all the resources are geared up to service that programme, you can make a great deal of money. If there is a disruption with the flying or the programme, that is when it becomes really expensive.

A classic example was long-haul business, which grew dramatically from 1994 to 1998. We bought in bigger 767 aircraft to handle the workload and in one year it became 25 per cent of our business.

Britannia's long-haul business from Gatwick to Australia celebrated ten years in November 1998. The airline's staff newspaper, Airwaves, *reported the event.*

Passengers on the first Perth/Adelaide flight of the winter season were treated to a buck's fizz reception and a slice of the 24-inch cake. The first charter airline to start flying down under with fortnightly flights from Luton to Perth and Cairns,

From the Airwaves *front cover: 10th anniversary Gatwick to Australia.*

BRITANNIA CELEBRATES 10 YEARS FLYING DOWN UNDER

Britannia celebrated 10 years flying to Australia from Gatwick Airport for tour operator, Ausbound, on 1st November. Passengers on the first Perth/Adelaide flight of the winter season were treated to a bucks fizz reception and a slice of the 24 inch cake, made especially for the big occasion. The first charter airline to start flying down under with fortnightly flights from Luton to Perth and Cairns, Britannia now has three flights a week to Brisbane, Melbourne, Perth and Adelaide plus a weekly flight to Auckland.

Celebrating 10 years flying down under are (L to R): Dawn Mitchell, Britannia's Station Manager for Gatwick, Shelley Jones, Britannia's Passenger Services Officer and Ausbound's Operations Manager, Jeremy Sweet.

Britannia now has three flights a week to Brisbane, Melbourne, Perth and Adelaide, plus a weekly flight to Auckland.

The mid 1990s saw the start of a unique relationship between Britannia and one of the world's foremost animal charities. The Born Free Foundation, founded as Zoo Check in 1984, was renamed in 1990 and officially established a year later. Its history went back to 1964, when Bill Travers and Virginia McKenna starred in the film Born Free, *which told the true story of George and Joy Adamson who returned Elsa the lioness to the wild and devoted their lives to the protection of lions and other species.* **Virginia McKenna** *explains the beginning of the relationship.*

Celebrations marking the 10th anniversary of the airline's flights to Australia welcomed passengers disembarking in Adelaide.

Our involvement with Britannia started in 1995, when the lion and lioness Raffi and Anthea were rescued from Tenerife. They, and Rikki the leopard who we rescued later, were kept in cages on the roof of a bar. We had spent almost five years trying to get them and it was only when the *Mail on Sunday* carried a major exposé of their pitiful existence that we succeeded.

Britannia carried the big cats in their crates back to the UK in one of their aircraft and, after two years at the Big Cat Sanctuary in Kent, flew them to Shamwari (a private game reserve in South Africa) to their new home in a huge bush enclosure. On the return journey the Cabin Crew asked me to join them in the galley, where they gave me wooden carvings of a lion and a lioness. They had had them specially made and I was extremely touched.

In 1996 Britannia flew Rikki the leopard from Tenerife back to the UK. In 1997 five tigers were rescued from an Italian circus trailer and flown back to the UK, and in 2000 two lions were rescued from a run-down zoo in Greece. In 1997 the airline started the 'Spare Coins Save Lives' in-flight appeal, which by the end of 2001 had raised more than £1 million. **Virginia McKenna** *has nothing but praise.*

I can't speak too highly of the airline. Britannia go to great lengths, over and above what is required, to ensure the cats' journey is smooth and trouble-free. Extra staff are laid on to guide us through unfamiliar countries and their regulations, and to liaise with officials at the various airports en route. There have never been any problems with transporting the animals. I am sure they don't much like

ABOVE Celebrities are heavily involved with Born Free and thus Britannia.
Absolutely Fabulous *star Joanna Lumley (left) is pictured with Virginia
McKenna at the naming of the aircraft* Bill Travers.

ABOVE RIGHT *Well-wishers gather round one of the big cats flown by Britannia
for the Born Free Foundation.*

LEFT Men Behaving Badly *star Martin Clunes, dressed as a female Cabin Crew
member, in an onboard video appeal for the Born Free Foundation.*

being kept in a crate in the belly of the aircraft but they invariably seem calm and unstressed. We always have our vet with them and Britannia very kindly allow him to access the hold via an internal chute.

From time to time the Captain will announce to the passengers that they have a lion, tiger or leopard on board and everyone is very pleased and excited when they hear about their unusual travelling companions!

We will always ask Britannia for help if they have any flights available. They are our first choice for these rescue flights and we are extremely grateful for their continued help and generosity.

Celebrities are heavily involved in Born Free and thus Britannia. The efforts of the airline staff and passengers helped rescue 15 chimpanzees and relocate them on a jungle island in the middle of Lake Victoria. The project was filmed by BBC Television and starred Nicholas Lyndhurst of Only Fools and Horses *fame. Joanna Lumley of* Absolutely Fabulous *is also a keen supporter of Born Free and has helped promote the Britannia Airways onboard appeal, as has* **Martin Clunes** *of* Men Behaving Badly, *who starred in an onboard video for the appeal. He later wrote to 'all the nice Britannia people'.*

Thanks very much for helping to make so much possible for the Born Free Foundation. The Spare Coins Save Lives in-flight collection has raised a staggering amount for Born Free and made thousands of pairs of trousers and handbags an awful lot lighter.

I do hope you are enjoying your end of this appeal as much as I enjoyed my end … if you know what I mean.

The airline introduced its 'Royal Service' in the early 1990s.

In the early 1990s Britannia launched its in-flight 'Royal Service', as **Helen Butler** *describes:*

It meant that for the first time we were putting branding on in-flight service. The meal tray had 'Royal Service' written on it; all the items were dark blue. The carpets were dark blue, the seats were dark blue and the headrest was red and blue. I'm not sure how we arrived at the name but the service existed for three or four years. It was an attempt to make the in-flight service more upmarket. I think we soon realised that it was a little pretentious and we were trying to be something we weren't. It had come about with the best of intentions but it looked as though we were trying to copy scheduled services.

By then I was General Manager, Marketing, and Roger Burnell asked me to develop a new in-flight service brand. It took some two years to develop and we had professional branding companies involved.

The result was 360, the new brand name of our in-flight service. We redid the interior of the aircraft using a basic lilac colour, which is bright and cheerful and has a good holiday feel about it. We branded all the meal trays, the in-flight entertainment and even the cocktail sticks were named.

We chose 360 because it actually has no meaning but it is memorable. The design was awarded a Certificate of Excellence in the European Design Annual Awards in 1999.

The branding was launched to the managers in March 1997, where the new uniforms – designed by Elizabeth Emanuel – were also displayed. During the next month some 1450 Cabin Crew visited the Hilton Hotel at Gatwick, where they were fitted for their new blue and red uniforms and trained in the new service. **Pedro Achillea**, *who flew as Cabin Crew with the airline for many years, and was Head of Cabin Services before taking on the role of looking after in-flight retail, takes up the story.*

I was responsible for the training of Cabin Crew in the new 360 service. The 'Royal Service' had been very traditional, not just in its name but in the look of the cabins, which was very austere and old fashioned.

The 360 service not only modernised the cabins but it gave the Cabin Crew the chance to become real people. We wanted them to let their own personalities come through and deliver a service that was fresher and more contemporary. I think perhaps the idea of the 360 logo was that it was all-encompassing, a complete service.

We were heavily involved in the new uniform design that Elizabeth Emanuel eventually produced. We were looking for a more informal uniform – away from the formal military 'Royal Service' look.

There were substantial changes in catering. We introduced things like afternoon tea, sausage and mash, roast beef on inbound flights on Sundays, and we themed menus for destinations. Not all the ideas were successful. Passengers didn't like afternoon tea – they preferred a hot meal.

A new logo and big changes on the catering front introduced the 360 service.

And to our surprise, some of the passengers did not like the 360 branding; they thought we were dumping the British feel about the airline.

Throughout the 1980s and early 1990s, Britannia continued in its ground-breaking medical research, largely through the efforts of **Dr Alan Roscoe**. *More than a decade of research into the workload of commercial pilots, using volunteer pilots like Captains Stu Grieve and Paul Watson as 'guinea pigs', provided data which could be of value to the design and ergonomics of future-generation flight decks, and was used by Boeing, NASA and the United States Air Force.*

Dr Roscoe also produced information and papers on 'cosmic radiation and the frequent flyer', emergency onboard medical kits, in-flight medical emergencies, medical fitness to travel by air and much more. On the airliner cabin environment he commented:

Many passengers are under the impression that the cabins of modern jet airliners are not as healthy as they should be. Passengers believe they suffer health problems when they fly because of the recirculated air in modern airliner cabins.

In fact the aircraft cabin is much healthier than most public rooms and ground-based transport and air quality compares favourably with hospital burns units and operating theatres.

For some passengers, the biggest problem with a holiday package is the basic fear of flying. In the early 1990s Britannia launched a 'flying with confidence' course. **Anthea Billington** *now runs the course at the airline's training centre at Castle Donington.*

The course was originally started as a commercial decision. Our customer relations department was getting calls from people who were afraid of flying. The only airline running a course was British Airways and we were referring our passengers to them. The Department Manager at the time, Tina Barbour, decided that maybe there was an opening for us, not only to help people to fly, but because these were potential Britannia and Thomson customers.

The main fear is claustrophobia, followed by people feeling they are not in control and fear of heights. Also, people who have been in severe turbulence are often very concerned.

The whole point of the course is for participants to achieve an hour's flying at the end of the day. There are usually between 75 and 85 people on the course and we have a lot of Britannia staff from all levels and departments who come along to help out on a volunteer basis.

New uniforms, designed by Elizabeth Emanuel, were launched in March 1997. She is pictured (centre) surrounded by Cabin Crew.

With the backdrop of a Boeing 757 turbine Lara Wilkinson (left), now Cabin Crew Regional Manager, North, and Heidi Bryn-Jacobson show off the new look.

We usually manage to get more than 95 per cent to take the hour's flight. We don't cure people, people cure themselves. It is very much their own strength of character that gets them through and helps them confront their own demons.

Dr Alan Roscoe *has plenty of praise for the course.*

It is without doubt one of the best of its type, and it is an important element of the course that people fly and that they fly in an airliner, which is the way they will travel.

Around 20 per cent of the population of the developed world are frightened of flying and some ten per cent avoid travelling by air because of that fear.

In 1997 Britannia published a book,[1] written by **Dr Alan Roscoe**, *in which he explains:*

Fear of flying is not confined to any particular type of personality – the timid or anxious person, or what might be termed the 'nervous individual' – but affects the internationally famous entertainer, the successful business executive and the leading politician. Several people who are well known for their risk-taking activities, such as mountaineers, professional boxers and explorers, suffer greatly when they fly, and many avoid flying altogether when other modes of travel are available.

European expansion for Britannia came about in 1997–98 with the formation in Germany of Britannia Airways GmbH, which employed 200 staff and started with two Boeing 767-300 aircraft, and with the acquisition of the Swedish airline Blue Scandinavia.

The Swedish acquisition came about when the Thomson Travel Group bought Fritidsresor Group, the number two tour-operating group in the Nordic region, and the deal included the airline. **Roger Burnell** *comments:*

The airline became a Britannia subsidiary. They were flying 757s, having had a mixed bag of some 20 different aircraft over a short period.

It all meant that by the end of 1998 Britannia had carried 8.2 million passengers with a fleet comprising 20 Boeing 757s and nine Boeing 767s.

---

1 *Flying with Confidence,* by Alan H. Roscoe. Published by Britannia Airways, 1997.

11. A great airline and a great business

BRITANNIA AIRWAYS IS THE WORLD'S leading holiday airline; from 1999 to 2001 it maintained position as number one airline for on-time departures. During the summer season it operates more than 30,000 flights from the UK and the Nordic region to 18 different countries, carrying millions of passengers to the sun. In 2000 the number exceeded ten million for the first time. The challenge for the airline that regularly receives awards, plaudits and praise, is to see that every passenger feels that his or her holiday really does start at the departure airport, and ends in a relaxed style on return to the UK.

The 'comfort factor' is achieved by a great deal of hard work, intelligence and common sense, and the need constantly to look ahead to ways of improving matters.

A passenger charter announced in January 2002 by the Vice-President of the European Commission (EC) **Loyola de Palacio,** *to improve air passenger rights, has come as no surprise to Britannia, which has long championed those rights and, genuinely, puts the passenger first in its policies.*

Too many Europeans have a bad surprise when checking in for their flight. We want to cut the number of passengers who suffer from denied boarding; our proposals will make this practice much less common. We want to protect passengers against cancellations of flights for which operators are responsible, particularly when unexpected and made at a late stage. Strengthening the rights of passengers will help restore their confidence in air travel.

Non-scheduled flights, including package holiday flights, have been excluded from the air passenger rights to date but Loyola de Palacio, who is in charge of energy and transport, now wants to see these airlines included in the new reinforced regulations. Both Bob Parker-Eaton and Britannia's Passenger Relations and Claims Manager, **Gary Parker***, have been involved with the EC proposals.*

Madame de Palacio is looking to be the consumers' champion for air travel. She means all modes of air travel, whether it be scheduled, chartered, domestic or international. Her plan includes being able to deliver the right prices, the right fare structure, the right information ahead of travelling, dealing with delays and a whole variety of matters affecting the passenger.

Britannia has always been involved in lobbying where legislation is likely to impact on the industry. This included the 'Keep Duty Free' campaign in 1999.

Considering in the UK we are carrying over eight million passengers, and there is inevitably the chance of upsetting them either outbound or inbound, the number of complaints we have is minimal. Including the most minor problems, our complaint ratio is better than one in 700.

We have now integrated customer services with Thomson and Lunn Poly to become a seamless group operation, which means communication is now much better, particularly as far as the customer is concerned. If, for instance, there has been a problem in the shop with selling the holiday, Lunn Poly can now ask us to add a little touch with a bottle of champagne on board or some other service which will show the customer that we recognise there has been a difficulty. It is the proactive side of customer services.

If there is a problem on the post-departure side, we have had a policy for a long while now that each complaint is dealt with as an individual matter. We don't just send out a cut and pasted letter or a standard response. Customers are more discerning nowadays and they know what to expect, and they do not want to be brushed off.

Britannia also carries out detailed passenger surveys from time to time, with some surprising results. In 1999 a press release revealed:

Men take fewer changes of underwear on holiday than women. The survey conducted on flights out of Manchester and Gatwick airports asked holidaymakers on their way to Spanish resorts questions about their habits and plans. Asked how many changes of underwear they had brought with them, the average number for men was 0.89 per night, compared with 1.2 pairs for women.

The holidaymakers, however, did take with them stocks of teabags, photos of loved ones and jars of Marmite and Bovril. They often forgot to take a toothbrush, cameras and film, batteries, electric razors and plug adaptors. They also missed their pets more than their family, as **Gary Parker** *reveals.*

I remember being called to a departure gate where there was a problem with a customer. He had brought his pet goldfish in a Tupperware box and wanted to take it on holiday but was concerned that it would have to go through the X-ray machine. We took it back to our office and looked after it until he returned from his holiday.

The worst thing that can happen to an airline occurred at 11.18am on 14 September 1999, when Boeing 757 G-BYAG en route from Cardiff crashed at Gerona and finished in a neighbouring field. It had 243 passengers and seven crew on board – 50 were taken to hospital. There were no fatalities. Director of Flight Safety **Captain Colin Sharples** *describes the incident:*

The aircraft was operating a holiday charter flight from Cardiff to Gerona in Spain. There was bad weather in the Pyrenees area of Spain as the aircraft approached and the first approach had to be discontinued. The aircraft landed very heavily after the second approach, bounced and on the second touchdown the nosewheel collapsed.

The aircraft veered right and came to rest in a muddy field adjacent to the airfield, breaking into three pieces.

The passengers were evacuated into the muddy field and eventually taken by coach to the terminal building. Those requiring medical treatment, including the Captain, were then transferred to hospital.

Staff from the airline and tour company were quickly assembled and sent to Gerona to give whatever assistance they could. Most passengers were not hurt and most of those hurt only had minor injuries, so the vast amount of passengers elected to stay in Spain and continue their holiday. However, as all personal belongings were trapped on the aircraft for several days, a great deal of assistance had to be given both financially and practically to ensure all our customers had the basic necessities of life. After about three or four days the accident investigation team at last cleared our team to go on board and collect the suitcases, handbags and items like spectacles, of which they found 60 pairs alone.

There was one lady passenger who said that she had lost a gold bracelet in the mud, worth some £35,000. She described exactly where it was; we went there and found it immediately.

The support operation lasted two weeks and, though emotionally draining for the staff involved, proved to be a great success.

The inquiry into the accident started immediately but as in all air accidents proved to be quite complex. A brief interim report was published in early 2000 but the detailed final report is still awaited.

Peter Buckingham *had taken over as Managing Director from Roger Burnell in July 1998.*

> *How has Britannia changed over the last 40 years? Quite simply it hasn't. Britannia is and will always be its people: it is not about colour schemes or interior fits – it's about people. I have spent 27 years working for an organisation that has constantly punched above its weight, and left me wondering why our staff care so much? The answer is simple. Britannia hasn't changed: we might have a new vision, mission and values but we are still the same, a family of people who can and do make a difference.*
>
> NICK WHITE
> Director Engineering and Maintenance

Love it or hate it, jars of Marmite figure in the stocks taken abroad by British holidaymakers for their breaks in the sun.

Managing Director Peter Buckingham: 'An airline has its own life.'

Initially there was a great deal of shock within the company over the accident. Then a great number of people volunteered to help in any way they could, including going out to the site to help passengers.

In the end there was a feeling of pride in the way we had dealt with the accident. We had handled it in a very professional way. The aircrew worked professionally, the backup teams worked professionally, the incident centre was operated professionally and all aspects of the machine swung into action properly.

Media Relations Manager **Russell Ison** *also praised the staff.*

When something big happens here there is an enormous camaraderie. Everybody wants to be involved – they don't want to be at home. This is their company and they want to help.

And in several other ways 1999 was proving a tough year, as **Peter Buckingham** *found.*

The group had floated in May 1998 and all our efforts had been directed towards that event. In 1997 we had to hit our targets and in 1998 we certainly had to hit our targets, and so we had taken some tough actions, like selling a flight simulator and outsourcing some work.

In 1999 things were proving very difficult. With the float anything left in the cupboard had gone, and there was no financial cushion. We had also been struggling with the operations and losing out on our on-time performance record. There was also a pilot shortage.

By 2000 things had improved. We had acted firmly in getting our costs down, we had sorted out the pilot shortage and our operational side was improving fast.

I always feel that an airline is like a human being. It has its own life and it works regardless of what is happening. Our passengers, of course, had no idea of the problems.

At the end of July 2000 the European Commission approved the takeover of the Thomson Travel Group by German group Preussag in a £1.8 billion deal. Preussag is the world leader in tourism. The group covers more than 80 per cent of the

> Over the years the combination of high quality training and exceptional customer care has proved a successful formula which we have stuck to. We still want our customers to be greeted by a smart and professional crew member as they would expect. However, they now expect so much more, therefore we have to be even more innovative and provide a better service than ever before.
>
> DAWN WILSON
> General Manager Cabin Services

European market and includes 3658 travel agencies, 75 tour operators and brands, 90 aircraft and around 270 hotels. Its customer base is around 22 million holiday-makers. Its global brand for tourism is the 'World of TUI'. At the time of the EU approval for the takeover, **Dr Michael Frenzel,** *Chairman of the Preussag management board, said:*

Like the TUI Group, Thomson has a strong market presence, a balanced brand portfolio and a high degree of integration across all links of the tourism value-added chain. With TUI Group and Thomson we have achieved a quantum leap towards the formation of the leading integrated tourism group.

Two months before the takeover **Kevin Hatton,** *then 55, started his retirement by moving to Florida with his wife. He had worked in aviation all his life and took early retirement after running the cargo side of British Airways for almost seven years, during which time it became the fifth largest freight carrier in the world.*

Executive Chairman TUI Northern Europe and Preussag Airlines Charles Gurassa helps promote the 'World of TUI' global image.

Shortly before I retired I was called by Charles Gurassa, now Executive Chairman TUI Northern Europe and Preussag Airlines, who mentioned the possibility of some potential opportunities at his group. But I decided that I had just had enough and I wanted to retire. The last few years with BA had been very tough, a lot of changes, a lot of industrial relations challenges.

In Florida I was out most days on my (overly powerful) jet ski and was having a wonderful time, when Charles called me again to say Thomson was now owned by Preussag and there would be a vacancy at Britannia Airways and was I interested? I consulted my family; my wife thought I was getting bored, which I don't think I was, but I came over and saw Charles. I also saw Dr Frenzel, and eventually I joined the airline in January 2001 and took over as Managing Director from Peter Buckingham.

Peter Buckingham moved to the Thomson headquarters, where he became Head of Group Integration. **Kevin Hatton** *knew Britannia well from his work in BA and other airlines.*

Amongst its peer group it had an outstanding reputation.

During his career **Kevin Hatton** *had worked for a while in the charter business with British Airtours but mostly his time had been with scheduled operators.*

I don't think there is a great deal of difference between charter and scheduled, certainly in terms of operational and professional abilities.

We clearly have to sweat the assets, we have to have three rotations a day on short-haul operations and items like that, but Britannia does not cut corners. In the hangars, on the flight deck, or with the Cabin Crew, it's perfectly obvious that the standards are very high indeed.

I suppose the major challenge is how we react in times of disruption. Unlike scheduled airlines in adversity we can't cancel flights; we have an obligation to bring customers back.

That really came to the forefront in June/July 2001, when we had the coach drivers' strike in the Balearic Islands. Some of the scheduled airlines just cancelled their flights but unlike them we could not just give the tickets back to our passengers and tell them to sort their own problems out.

There is a great complexity in solving those problems. Some passengers decided not to fly out in the first place and needed information and help on dealing with their own insurance matters.

There also needs to be considerable liaison with, in this case, Lunn-Poly, with the resorts, with the incident room at Thomson and with the incident room at Britannia. I must say, the whole matter was handled very well indeed; I was very, very impressed with the efficiency.

And **Russell Ison** *recalls the efforts made to help passengers.*

We were putting as many staff as we could out to airports in the UK to deal with the Thomson and Britannia passengers. I went with Kevin Hatton to Gatwick for more than 24 hours, Gary Parker went to Stansted and the other airports were all covered. Britannia people abandoned their normal jobs to help out; we finished with some 20 staff at Gatwick, for instance. Compared with our competitors we went that little bit further to help and although the passengers were pretty upset by the delays caused by the strike, they did appreciate the fact that we were there. We did not simply rely on our handling agents at the airports to sort out the problems.

ABOVE The tailplane logo, affectionately known in the airline as the 'old lady in a wheelchair' goes from the new look 'World of TUI' global image adopted by Britannia Airways.

RIGHT Having been the first airline in Europe to fly the 737 in its early days, the airline took delivery of two next-generation Boeing 737-800s in 2000.

The biggest difficulty was getting information to the passengers. There were tens of thousands of people there and the PA system ceases to be any use because people take no notice or can't hear properly, and once they have checked in they move off to the bar or restaurant or waiting areas and it is very hard to get them all together. On the islands themselves Thomson Holidays had made efforts to book as many taxis as possible to get people to their hotels. We laid on children's entertainment. At Palma one of our staff went to a pizza house and ordered 100 pizzas; another ordered 1000 sandwiches from a store, and these places stayed open all night so that the holidaymakers stuck at the airport had something to eat.

We think our efforts were appreciated by the majority of the passengers and the airports were also pleased that we had managed to ease some of the pain for them.

I joined Britannia HR Division in April 1988 and walked into a world which, in my eyes, was behind the times in terms of business practice and HR. Thankfully this did not last long. Britannia people on the other hand were, and still are today, professional, fun and loyal to the airline.

Change came in 1989 with the acquisition of Orion, and other initiatives such as 'Flight Plan for the 90s' and the birth of a new airline in 1997 in Germany which followed. I was fortunate to be part of the project team that established the German airline within 5 months – the first flight being from Schoenfeld Berlin November 1997, and sadly its demise in 2001.

CATHY HINDES
Human Resources Manager (Air)

For **Kevin Hatton,** *the problems took a turn for the worse at Gatwick when two 767s went unserviceable.*

We had a particularly interesting group of passengers, and once they found out I was in the building I finished up with a police escort. I found that in this particular case the passengers most in need of care and attention – the families and the elderly – were most understanding but some of the others were not. There was a degree of selfishness and a lack of understanding that did not help matters.

But we did our best and it was all sorted in the end, and we had very few formal complaints in later weeks.

It is part of **Kevin Hatton's** *style not to spend all his time in an office.*

I like to get out and see what is really happening. I am not in any way dismissive of the line managers but it is important to see the work at the sharp end, the flight deck, cabin and operations, and also to understand what is happening behind the scenes.

Palma, the airline's first-ever destination, is Britannia's busiest airport outside the UK, with more than 100 flights a week in the summer, and its Station Manager is **Sharon Davies.**

I have a small team in Britannia uniform who are here specifically to help passengers, as well as a behind-the-scenes team who keep things ticking over.

The main problem for us and our passengers is the size of the airport; it was opened in 1997 and is very, very big. I have now persuaded Britannia to provide me with a scooter so that I can get around quicker.

Another key factor for us is the turnaround time for flights and we have been working very hard on improving that side of operations. It is now (November 2001) brilliant and we have exceeded our targets. Our handling agents are Iberia and they have brought in some young dynamic chaps who have really got things moving, and I feel that we are really getting things right now.

The sheer volume of traffic coming in and out of Palma causes problems but we are up to speed and know how to handle the operation.

Palma probably sees more than its fair share of youngsters going to or coming from a holiday and who have over-celebrated. But for **Sharon Davies***, there is also another problem.*

I think our main passenger drinking problem is some of the women from the cruise ships. They can certainly be the worse for wear. The lads are alright. You do get the odd one or two, but on the whole they do as we ask. We tell them to calm down and behave themselves and they do.

Sharon Davies *is five feet five inches tall but together with a colleague, Chris Baynes, she is perfectly able to handle the young drinkers.*

Chris pulls her glasses down on her nose and treats them like their mum. They do as she says. We make it clear that if they are drunk they won't board the aircraft, so they usually drink some coffee and sober up. Generally they are all good lads, full of the chat, but only after a bit of fun.

In August 2001 the Preussag Group brought Britannia and Thomson Holidays under its umbrella 'World of TUI' global brand for tourism with a new logo that incorporates a smile. **Charles Gurassa***, Executive Chairman TUI Northern Europe and Preussag Airlines, explained:*

For all our millions of customers, our job is simply to give them the best weeks of their year – to make them smile – time and time again.

Sharon Davies has persuaded Britannia to provide her with a scooter for faster travel round the massive Palma Airport.

People want to travel with a company they trust, which has the right values and will really deliver what it promises. The smile represents all those things and we expect that it will become one of the best-known marks of quality and good service.

Charles Gurassa *moved from British Airways to become the then Chief Executive of Thomson Travel Group and one of his first visits was to Luton Airport to meet his Britannia Airways team.*

I went there to meet Peter Buckingham, then Managing Director, and the management team, and they took me through a presentation on their company, how it was run and what were the major issues.

They came across as a very professional group of experienced airline executives. It felt like a good team and a team with some real strength and depth.

It ran a great operation but it needed to become more competitive because the environment had become more competitive, and my focus was to ensure that what was a great airline also became a great business.

Thomson has no formal agreement to put its business through Britannia but clearly, as we have purchased the aircraft assets, we are not going to encourage Thomson to put the work with other people and leave our assets unused. But the risk in that strategy is that the in-house supplier can perceive themselves as not having to really compete for the business. The challenge at my level and at the Britannia level is to realise that the business will not come automatically.

It is essential that for Britannia to succeed and grow it offers not just the appropriate quality of product, operational robustness and stability, but is able to offer it at a price that is competitive in the market.

Britannia offers a very good service but again, this is a competitive world and the customers rightly expect good service; they don't expect to be treated poorly. They expect the 'planes to leave on time, they expect them to be clean and safe, they expect the crew to be friendly, where appropriate to have onboard food, onboard shopping and in-flight entertainment. The flight is part of the holiday experience and we want them to feel that Britannia is the best way to start and finish their holiday.

Aviation has changed over the last 40 years and consequently Britannia has changed with it. Air travel is far more common yet despite this increase in traffic, it is safer statistically than ever before. Better training of pilots, improved ground facilities and more sophisticated aircraft have combined to achieve this. The UK charter industry has been led by Britannia in these areas with its up-to-date equipment and training methods for pilots. These changes have seen Britannia pilots become skilled management professionals in a highly focused modern business.

CHRIS TURNER
Chief Pilot

Ground staff meet the Queen at the opening of the new terminal building at London Luton Airport on 25th November 1999.

That is happening. Britannia is clearly, from all the independent research, the best charter airline in the UK; be it from the Civil Aviation Authority punctuality statistics, be it from *The Daily Telegraph* consumer survey, Britannia is the benchmark – which is terrific and we are very proud of that but not complacent.

'The World of TUI' global image is important for Thomson and for Britannia and for all our companies. It links our tour operators, our airlines, our hotels, our travel agents and our coaches, because we want our customers to know they are part of a company that looks after them all the way from the time they book to the time they come home. It means new livery for our aircraft, not just those in the UK, but in our sister companies, and they will all have the same look and feel.

It was never our intention to change the name of the airline; it's a great brand, customers and staff like it, but the image needed to be updated and improved, which is why it will become part of TUI but retain the Britannia name.

I have flown with Britannia on many occasions. I think the flight crew are very professional and the Cabin Crew are fantastic. They love what they do, as do those behind the scenes, and it shows, and I am very proud to be part of that.

Index

Page references in **bold** relate to illustrations.

Achillea, Pedro (Head of Cabin Services) 89–90
Adamson, George and Joy 86
The Aeroplane 2, 26
affinity flights 52
Air 2000 81
Air Europe 62, 81
Air Transport Licensing Board (ATLB) 10, 12
Airbus 63, 65, 82–3, 83
aircraft *see* Boeing, Britannia, Constellation, York
Airwaves magazine 85–6, **85**
Airworthiness Requirements Board (ARB) 13
Alderman, Jamie (Pilot) 19, 27
Allen, Marianne (Chief Stewardess) 4, 7, **7**
Arab–Israeli war 52
ARB *see* Airworthiness Requirements Board
Atkinson, Captain Eric 47, **47**
ATLB *see* Air Transport Licensing Board
Australia, flights to 74, 85–6, **85**, **86**
Avro York *see* York

BA *see* British Airways
BAC One-Eleven 36–7, 38, 48–9
Bamberg, Harold (Chairman, British Eagle) 39, 47
Barbour, Tina (Department Manager) 90
Barnes, Terry and Iris 73, **73**
Barnett, John 47–8
Barnwell Memorial Lecture 38
Batten, Jean **67**, 68
Baynes, Chris 101
BEA *see* British European Airways
Berney, Henry M. 15–16
Berrisford, George (Performance and Navigation Manager) 63
Bill Travers (aircraft) iii, **87**
Billington, Anthea (secretary) 57–8, 83, 90, 92
'Black Wednesday' 85
BOAC *see* British Overseas Airways Corporation
Boeing 707 50, **51**, 52
Boeing 737
   and Britannia 34, 36, **37**, 43, **45**, 47, 48–9, 50
   disposal of 82
   features **43**, **45**, 55, 58, 60, **61**, **79**, 81, 83
   leasing 55, **55**, 57
   number 47, 56, 57, 73, 80
Boeing 737-200 34, **35**, **37**, 54, 65, 82, 98
Boeing 737-800 **99**
Boeing 747 65
Boeing 757 63, 81–3, **91**, 92
   view from **64**
Boeing 767
   acquisition 63, 73, 85
   features **61**, 65, 74, **75**, 83, 100
   number 73, 80, 92
   under construction 70, **71**

Born Free Foundation iii, 86, **87**, 88
Bowden, Billy (engineer) **46**
Bray, Roger 77
Brett, Captain Bill 24–5
Bristol Britannia *see* Britannia
Britannia (aircraft)
   as benchmark 103
   crew 42
   future 33–4
   introduction **25**, 27
   number 47
   phasing out 50
Britannia 102 21, 26, 33, 34
Britannia 312 21
Britannia Airways
   and Air Europe 62
   Boeing 707 50, **51**, 52
   Boeing 737 34, 36, **37**, 43, **43**, **45**, 47, 48–9, 50, **55**
   Boeing 767 63, 65, 73, 86
   and Court Line 54
   development 26, 33–4, 39–40, 47, 98
   engineers **46**
   jigsaw **44**
   logo 68
   naming 21
   and Thomson Organisation 29–30, 32–3
   see also specific aircraft
Britannia Airways GmbH 92
British Aircraft Corporation *see* BAC
British Airways (BA) 56, 90, 92
British Eagle 39, 47
British European Airways 10, 56
British Overseas Airways Corporation (BOAC) 16, 56
British United Airways (BUA) 7–8, 36, 48–9
Brooks, Ernie (engineer) **46**
Brown, David (Flight Engineer) 2, 4
Brown, Frank (Pilot) 6, 13
Brown, Peter (Financial Director) 72
Brunton, Gordon (Group Development Director)
   and BAC One-Eleven 36–7, 38
   and Boeings 34, 36, 63
   consolidation 33–4, 49
   departure 70
   diversification 29, 30, **31**, 32–3
   Ljubljana crash 41–2
Bryn-Jacobsen, Heidi (Cabin Crew) **91**
BUA *see* British United Airways
Buckingham, Peter (Managing Director) 95–6, **96**, 97, 102
Burnell, Roger (Managing Director)
   appointment 81, **81**
   Fritidsresor Group 92
   in-flight service 89
   profitability 85
   strategic review 82
   strike action 83
Butler, Helen (General Manager, Marketing) 73, **74**, 88–9
Buxton, Bill (Technical Director) 72–3

Cabin Crew
   Boeings 45, **51**, 52, 74
   Britannia 42
   duties **45**, 60, 66
   fund raising iii
   qualifications for 42
   and strike action 83
   uniform **13**, **14**, **53**, 56, 60, 66, 68, 89, **91**
'cardboard bomber' 43, **43**
Castle Donington training centre 90
Chalmers, Judith 56
Chamberlin, Joe (engineer) **46**
Christian, Brian (Commercial Director) 74
Civil Aviation Authority 42, 63, 103
Clarksons 49, 50, 52
Clayton, Jacky (Chief Stewardess) 41–3, **41**, **42**, 58, 60, 62, 66
Clunes, Martin iii, **87**, 88
coaches 9, 83, 98
Constellation
   emergencies 20, 25
   Euravia **5**, 7, **13**, 15
   features 27
   maintenance 26
   pilot training 13
   test flights 2
   withdrawal from service 21, 22, 33
   see also G-AHEN *etc.*
Constellation 049 1, 2, 4, **5**, 7, 16, 17–20
Court Line 36, 48, 52–4, 77
crashes 40–1, 94–6
Crosland, Tony (President, Board of Trade) 36, 37
Culver, Mike (General Manager Operations) 98
currency restrictions 36, 38
Cushion, Jim (engineer) **46**
customer services 94; *see also* passengers

Davies, Sharon (Station Manager, Palma) 100–1, **101**
Davison, Derek (Managing Director)
   appointments **7**, 39, 57, 62, 70, 72
   as Pilot 1, 2, 7, 25, **59**
   and Boeings 43, 44, 63, 70, **71**
   and Britannia 22
   flight crew training 43
   and International Thomson 72, 74
   Ljubljana crash 41
   and malpractice 6
   operational division 39–40
   plans for Luton Airport 46
   retirement of Jacky Clayton **42**
   and secretaries 57
   takeover of Skyways 19
de Palacio, Madame Loyola 93
Donaldson Airlines 26, 58
Douglas, David (Catering Manager) 43
duty free facilities 76, **93**

Eagleton, Margaret (uniform) **53**
Eastaff, Terri (uniform) 66, 68
Eastbury, Suzanne (First Officer) **67**
Easterbrook, Bob (Director, Gatwick Airport) 14

Edwards, Captain Peter 1–2, **1**
Edwards, Sir George (Managing Director, BAC) 36, 37
Edwards Committee 47
Emanuel, Elizabeth 89, **91**
emergencies 20, 22, 24–5, 42
engineers 46
ERM *see* Exchange Rate Mechanism
Euravia
    Constellations **5**, 7, **13**, 15
    early history 1–2, **1**, 4, **5**, 8, 9, 15
    engineering department 26
    finances 16–18, 20
    ground handling 14–15, 27
    livery **5**
    operations, 1962–3 18
    Operations Manual 6
    renaming 21–2
    takeover of Skyways 19
    York **15**
Exchange Rate Mechanism (ERM) 85

Falla, Jo (Cabin Crew) **19**
fear of flying 90, 92
Finnegan, Sid (Chief Engineer) 4
first day cover **68**
Flight International articles 10, 12, 15–16, 38, 40
'Flight Plan for the 90s' 81, 100
Forster, Mike (Chief Flight Engineer) 2, 42, 44
Frenzel, Dr Michael (Chairman, Pruessag) 97
Fritidsresor Group 92

G-AHEN 15, 22, **22**, 24–5
G-ANBA 33
G-ANBB 33, 40–1
G-ANBF 33
G-ANBJ **25**
G-ANBL 33
G-ANBO **31**, 33
G-ARVP 1, 15
G-ARXE 15
G-AVRL *Sir Ernest Shackleton* **37**, 38, 44
G-AYSI 50
G-BGYL *Jean Batten* **67**
G-BKPW *Earl Mountbatten of Burma* **68**, **69**, 73
G-BKVZ *Sir Winston Churchill* 73
G-BYAG 94–5
Garrett, Ian (Managing Director, Hallmark) 47–8, 53, 83–4
Gatwick Airport iii, 13, 14–15, 58, 62, 82, 94, 98
Ginns, Bob (Project Manager) 62, 63, 65, 82–3
Glass, Jamie 14–15
Graham, Martha 19, 20
Grainger, Pat (Cabin Crew) **19**
Grieve, Captain Stu 90
Gurassa, Charles (Chief Executive, Thomson Travel Group) 97, **97**, 101–2

Hadj, flights for 74
Hallmark Executive Travel Services 47–8, 53–4, 55, 83–4, **84**
Hamilton, Alan 43–4

Hankin, Ray 54
Harrington, Captain Jackie (Director) 4, 6
Harrington, Ted 14
Harrison, Elizabeth (Chief Stewardess) 41
Hatton, Kevin (Managing Director) ii, **ii**, 97–8, 100
Heathrow Airport 16, 18
Hessey, Ernest (Operations Manager) 4
Higgins, Francis (Managing Director, Thomson Holidays) 55
Hindes, Cathy (Human Resources Manager (Air)) 101
Hopkins, Captain Dave (Chairman)
    appointments 68, 70, 76, 81
    as Pilot 68, 70, 73, 80
    naming ceremony **69**
    presentation on aircraft use 70
    takeover problems 77–8
Horizon Holidays 9, 29, 32–3, 49, 77, 81
Hough, Captain John 84

Ideal Clothiers (uniform) 68
International Aircraft Cabin Safety Symposium 78
International Leisure Group 77, 81
International Thomson 70, 72
Ison, Russell (Media Relations Manager) 96, 98, 100
Israel Aircraft Corporation 21
Israeli Aircraft Industries, Lod 16

jigsaw **44**

'Keep Duty Free' campaign **93**
Kennedy, President John F. 8
King, Herdis (Senior Training Stewardess) 56
Kirk, Gill (Cabin Crew) **13**, **14**
Knatchbull, Philip and Timothy **69**

Laker, Freddie (Managing Director, British United Airways) 8
Langton, 'Captain' Ted
    airport facilities 14
    collaboration with Jed Williams 10, **11**
    diversification of Thomson Organisation 29, 32–3
    and Euravia 9, 21
    financial pressures 20
    Universal Sky Tours 9–10, 40
Lawson, Nigel (Chancellor of the Exchequer) 77
Leslie Whitley (uniform) 68
licences 10, 12
Little, Jimmy (Technical Director) 36, 39, 40, 62, 64
Ljubljana Airport crash 40–2
Llewellyn, Bryan 49, 50, 57
Lloyd, Sue (Cabin Crew) 34, **35**, **53**
Lockheed Constellation *see* Constellation
Lumb, Michael 26
Lumley, Joanna iii, **87**, 88
Lunn-Poly 81, 83, 94, 98
Luton Airport
    and Boeings 43, **43**, 52, 73
    Constellation at **5**
    cost of using 82
    and Euravia 1, 14–15
    flying club 7, 20

ground handling 28, 66
    plans for 46
    terminal building **11**, **103**
    visit of Charles Gurassa 102
Luton Borough Council 46
Lyndhurst, Nicholas 88

Macmillan, Harold (Prime Minister) 8
Manchester Airport 1, 50, 82, 94
Manchester Airport Agencies (Servisair) 26–7
Marmite **95**
Marshalls of Cambridge 16
McDougall, Captain Roy (Director)
    appointments 4, 6–7, 62
    and ARB examination 13
    award **23**
    and Boeing 707 50, **51**, 52
    and 'Hen' (G-AHEN) 22, 24–5
    and malpractice 6
McKenna, Virginia iii–iv, **iii**, 86, **87**, 88
meals 4, 42, 43, 74, 89, **89**
medical research 78, 90
Ministry of Defence 39, 48–9
Moss, Jack (Manager, In-Flight Services) 64
Mountbatten, Countess **69**
Muckleston, Bob (Financial Director)
    appointments 26, 39, 62
    delivery of Boeing 737 44, 46
    disposal of aircraft 33
    financial affairs 16–18, **17**, 20–1
    leasing of Boeing 737 55
    and Skyways 17–18

Newton, Bernard (Technical Director) 58, 62, 72–3, **72**, 83
Nobbs, Eric 26–8

Offchocks newsletter 68
OPEC *see* Organisation of Petroleum Exporting Countries
Organisation of Petroleum Exporting Countries (OPEC) 52, 57
Orion 77, 80–2, 100

package holiday industry 29
Parakh, Rusi (Flight Engineer) 44
Parker, Gary (Passenger Relations and Claims Manager) 93–4, 98
Parker-Eaton, Bob (Director)
    appointment 62
    arrival at Britannia 54
    and Boeing 767 65–6, **75**
    design of uniform 66
    naming ceremony 68
    and passenger 78, 80, 93–4
    retirement of Jacky Clayton **42**
    trooping contract 48–9
Parkins, Geoff (Technical Director) 58, 72
passengers
    behaviour 78, 80, 101
    coach drivers' strike 98, 100

facilities **74, 79**
health problems 90
luggage 94, **95**
miles 34
problems 100
rights 93
Pennington, Captain Nick 73
pets 94
Pollock, Jill (Cabin Crew) **19**
Preussag Group 96–7, 101

Queen Elizabeth II **103**

Raitz, Vladimir 9–10, 29–30, 32–3, 77
Redding, Robert 65
Reed, Arthur 47
Rhodes, Ann (Cabin Crew) 66, 68
Ringway Airport *see* Manchester Airport
Riviera Holidays 30, 33
Robertson, Jock (engineer) **46**
Rome emergency 24–5
Roscoe, Dr Alan (Chief Medical Officer) 78, 90, 92
'Royal Service' 88–9, **88**
Rushton, Peter (Commandant, Gatwick Airport) 14

safety training 42
Sauvage, John (Managing Director)
    appointments 39, **39**, 57
    and Bob Parker-Eaton 54
    and Britannia 39–40, 44
    Ministry of Defence contracts 48–9
Searles, Terry (engineer) **46**
Sharples, Captain Colin (Director of Flight Safety) 95
Skyways 2, **15**, 16
'Spare Coins Save Lives' iii, 86, 88
strikes 83, 98
Swift, Peter (Projects Manager) 34, 36
Tanner, Bruce 77
Tanton, Captain Don
    and Boeings 43, 44, 50, 52
    and Britannia 102 22
    and Constellation 7–8, 19–20, **19**
    and Euravia 2, 4, 6–7
    in cockpit **3**
    and Lord Thomson **32**

Tanton, Nigel (Pilot) **3**
tax free gifts 76, **76**
Thatcher, Margaret (Prime Minister) 62, 77
Thomas, Lord (Chairman, BOAC) 39, 40, 52, 62
Thomas, Sir Miles *see* Thomas, Lord
Thomson, Lord
    and Board of Trade 37
    diversification 29–30, **31**
    and Don Tanton **32**
    flights with Britannia 49
    oversight of Britannia Airways 40
    price regulation 47
Thomson, Roy *see* Thomson, Lord
Thomson Holidays 50, 70, 81, 101
Thomson Organisation
    acquisition of Horizon 70, 77
    and Boeing 767 63
    diversification 29
    inclusive tour flights 47
    integration of Britannia 44
    scholarships 41
Thomson Travel
    crew transportation 83–4, **84**
    flights to Australia 74
    long-term projections 63
    management 49
    percentage of flying 85
    recovery programme 55
    success 49
    takeover by Preussag 96–7
'360' service 89, **89**
The Times 47
Transavia 55, 57
Travel Trade Gazette 28, 40
TravelNews 54–5
Travers, Bill 86; *see also* Bill Travers
Turner, Chris (Chief Pilot) 73, 102

uniforms **14**, **53**, 56, 60, 66, 68, 89, **91**
United Airlines 65
Universal Sky Tours
    and Britannia Airways 20, 29
    financial control 30
    foundation 9–10
    growth 34

licences 12
resignation of Ted Langton 40
and Thomson Organisation 29–30

'Wanderer' flights 56
Wanderer magazine 56, **56**
Watret, Jim (Pilot) 52
Watson, Captain Paul 90
Weedon, John (engineer) **46**
Weeks, Roger 66
Wheatcroft, Steve (consultant) 36
White, Nick (General Manager Maintenance Services) 95
Whittle, Sir Frank **69**
Wilkinson, Lara (Cabin Crew Resource Manager North) **91**
Williams, Jed (Managing Director)
    and BOAC 21
    and Bob Muckleston 17
    and Boeing 737 34, 36, 38
    and Britannia airliners 33–4
    diversification 30
    and Euravia 9, 14, 18, 21
    financial pressures 15, 20
    and jet flight 26
    licences to fly 10, 12
    retirement 39–40
    and Ted Langton 10, **11**
Williams, John Ernest Derek *see* Williams, Jed
Williamson, Willie 22
Wilson, Dawn (General Manager Cabin Services) 96
Wilson, Harold (Prime Minister) 36
Wilson, T. (Chairman, Boeing) 70, **71**
winter flights 74
winter holidays 57
'World of TUI' ii, 97, **97**, **99**, **101**, 103
Worth, Helen iii

Yemen Airways 55, **55**
Yenne, Bill 65
York (aircraft) **15**, 16, 18, 26, 33
Young, Lord (Trade Secretary) 77

Zoo Check 86